Please return this book on or before the date shown above. To renew go to www.essex.gov.uk/libraries, ring 0845 603 7628 or go to any Essex library.

Essex County Council

Please Note

Although every care has been taken with the production of this book to ensure that any projects, designs, modifications and/or programs, etc., contained herewith, operate in a correct and safe manner and also that any components specified are normally available in Great Britain, the Publishers and Author do not accept responsibility in any way for the failure (including fault in design) of any project, design, modification or program to work correctly or to cause damage to any equipment that it may be connected to or used in conjunction with, or in respect of any other damage or injury that may be so caused, nor do the Publishers accept responsibility in any way for the failure to obtain specified components.

Notice is also given that if equipment that is still under warranty is modified in any way or used or connected with home-built equipment then that warranty may be void.

© 2009 BERNARD BABANI (publishing) LTD

First Published – January 2009

Essex County Council Libraries

British Library Cataloguing in Publication Data:

A catalogue record for this book is available from the British Library

ISBN 978-0-85934-701-3

Cover Design by Gregor Arthur

Printed and bound in Great Britain for Bernard Babani (publishing) Ltd

Preface

Microsoft Excel is the world's leading spreadsheet program; it's essential software for anyone working with tables of data and needing to produce graphs and charts. This book is intended to help newcomers to spreadsheets to learn the basic skills, using simple, clear, everyday examples. A step-by-step approach is used, developed over the author's many years of teaching.

Early chapters in the book show what you can do with Excel and introduce the latest version, Excel 2007, with its Tabbed Ribbon and radical new way of working compared with earlier software.

The book then gets down to the basic tasks of entering data, performing calculations, saving spreadsheet files and printing on paper. Jargon is avoided wherever possible but where necessary it's explained in the text and in the Glossary at the end of the book. The ease with which spreadsheets can be edited by amending data and inserting and deleting rows and columns is then discussed, together with formatting in different styles and colours to make spreadsheets more attractive and readable.

Excel 2007 makes the drawing of eye-catching pie charts and column and line graphs a simple task anyone can quickly master. Professional-looking charts can greatly enhance a report or presentation and creating these is explained in detail. The use of Excel 2007 for creating a name and address database which can be sorted and filtered is also discussed.

Later chapters explain basic file management tasks, such as organizing, copying, moving and deleting files. Spreadsheets saved as files on disc may contain important financial or personal data and it's essential that these files are managed efficiently and securely. Looking after your computer and its data files using effective but inexpensive procedures is discussed in detail.

Although Excel 2007 was used in the preparation of this book, users of earlier versions of Excel and other spreadsheet software should also find much of the material helpful.

About the Author

Jim Gatenby trained as a Chartered Mechanical Engineer and initially worked at Rolls-Royce Ltd using computers in the analysis of jet engine performance. He obtained a Master of Philosophy degree in Mathematical Education by research at Loughborough University of Technology and taught mathematics and computing in school for many years before becoming a full-time author. His most recent teaching posts included Head of Computer Studies and Information Technology Coordinator. The author has written many books in the fields of educational computing and Microsoft Windows, including many of the titles in the highly successful Older Generation series from Bernard Babani (publishing) Ltd.

The author has considerable experience of teaching students of all ages and abilities, in school and in adult education. For several years he successfully taught the well-established CLAIT course and also GCSE Computing and Information Technology.

Trademarks

Microsoft, Windows, Windows XP, Windows Vista, Office 2007, Word and Excel are either trademarks or registered trademarks of Microsoft Corporation. Norton AntiVirus and Norton 360 are trademarks of Symantec Corporation. F-Secure Internet Security is a trademark or registered trademark of F-Secure Corporation. AVG Anti-Virus is a trademark or registered trademark of AVG Technologies. nero-BURNING ROM is a trademark of Ahead Software AG. All other brand and product names used in this book are recognized as trademarks or registered trademarks, of their respective companies.

Acknowledgements

I would like to thank my wife Jill and our son David for their help and support during the writing of this book.

Contents

1

Introducing Spreadsheets   1

What is a Spreadsheet   1
Advantages of Spreadsheets   2
Graphs and Charts   3
Spreadsheet Applications   4
Totalling Rows and Columns   4
Multiplying Two Columns Together   5
Calculation of BMI – Multiplication and Division   6
Managing Lists of Names and Addresses   7
Summary of Spreadsheet Advantages   8

2

Introducing Excel 2007   9

Excel 2007 and Microsoft Office 2007   9
Installing Excel 2007   10
Multiple Installations from a Single Office CD   10
The Product Key   10
Activation   12
Launching Excel from the All Programs Menu   12
Launching Excel from the Start Menu   13
Launching Excel from an Icon on the Desktop   13
The Excel 2007 Screen   14
The Excel 2007 Ribbon   14
The Office Button   15
The Home Tab   16
The Insert Tab   17
The Formulas Tab   17
Worksheets and Workbooks   18

3

Entering Labels, Numbers and Formulas 19

Moving Around in a Worksheet   19
Moving Down a Column   19
Moving Along a Row   20
Moving to a Specified Cell   20
Cell Contents   21
Entering Labels into a Cell   21
Widening a Column   21
Entering Numbers   22
Entering a Formula   22
Displaying the Formula in a Calculated Cell   23
Totalling Rows and Columns – the SUM Function   24
Multiplying Two Cells Together   25
Editing a Cell at a Later Date   26
Functions   26

4

Creating, Saving and Printing 27

Entering the Labels and Headings   28
Entering the Numbers   28
Calculated Cells – Totalling a Column   29
Replication   30
Displaying the Formulas in All Calculated Cells   30
Totalling Along a Row   31
Replicating a Formula Down a Column   32
Using the Average Function   33
Saving a Spreadsheet   34
Printing a Spreadsheet   36
Portrait or Landscape   36
Printing Gridlines   37
Displaying and Printing Formulas   37
Exercise 1: Creating a Spreadsheet and Entering Data   38
and Formulas

5

Editing and Formatting 39
Editing the Cell Contents 39
Editing in the Cell 39
Editing in the Formula Bar 39
Deleting a Row 40
Deleting a Column 41
Recovering from Mistakes – the Undo Feature 41
Inserting a New Row 42
Inserting a New Column 43
Exercise 2: Editing a Spreadsheet 44
Formatting a Spreadsheet 45
Selecting Cells for Formatting or Editing 46
Formatting Numbers 47
Exercise 3: Formatting a Spreadsheet 49
Checklist of Spreadsheet Skills 50

6

Excel Graphs and Charts 51
Introduction 51
Types of Chart, Pie Chart, Line Graph, Column Chart 52
Drawing a Pie chart 53
Pie Chart Styles 55
Updating a Chart 57
Saving a Graph or Chart 57
Drawing a Line Graph 58
Selecting Two Non Adjacent Columns 59
Formatting a Chart 61
Two Lines on One Chart 62
Drawing a Column Chart 63
Changing to a Different Type of Chart 65
Drawing a Clustered Column Graph 66
Printing a Chart 67
Inserting an Excel Chart into a Report 68
Exercise 4: Excel Graphs and Charts 70

7

Using Excel as a Database 71
Introduction 71
Creating an Address File in Excel 72
Entering the Data 72
Saving the File of Names and Addresses 73
Sorting into Order 74
Using an Excel Filter 75
Find & Select 76
Using Excel as a Data Source 77
Printing Name and Address Lables 78

8

Managing Excel Files 79
Saving an Excel File 79
Creating a New Folder 80
File Types 80
Locating an Excel File 81
Viewing Files in the Computer Window 82
Common File Management Tasks 83
Right-Click Menus 83
Properties of an Excel File 85
Read Only Files 86
Hidden Files 86

9

Safety Precautions 87
Introduction 87
Making Regular Backups 88
Backup Media 88
Checking that a Backup File is Retrievable 88
CD Writing or "Burning" 89
Using Windows Vista's CD/DVD Burning Software 89
Checking the Files on a Backup CD 93

The USB Flash Drive or Memory Stick   94
Recovering Files from a Flash Drive or CD   95
Disk Cleanup – Removing Redundant Files   97
Using Disk Defragmenter   100
System Restore   102
Windows Update   103
Summary: Safety Precautions   104

10

External Threats to Your Excel Files   105
Introduction   105
The Windows Security Centre   106
The Windows Firewall   107
Turning Windows Firewall On   107
Automatic Updating   108
Malware Protection   110
Norton 360   111
AVG Anti-Virus   112
Wireless Network Security   113
Summary: External Threats to Your Excel Files   114

Glossary   115

Index   117

Keyboard Shortcuts

Microsoft Office programs such as Excel provide a set of keyboard shortcuts, used as an alternative to the mouse and menus to carry out common tasks. Keyboard shortcuts for some of the most commonly used Excel operations are listed below. **CTRL+B**, for example, means "while holding down the **CTRL** key press the **B** key".)

CTRL+A	Select the entire worksheet.
CTRL+B	Apply or remove bold formatting.
CTRL+C	Copy selected cells to the clipboard, a temporary store in the memory.
CTRL+G	Displays the **Go To** dialogue box.
CTRL+I	Applies or removes italics.
CTRL+N	Creates a new, blank workbook.
CTRL+O	Displays the **Open** dialogue box.
CTRL+P	Displays the **Print** dialogue box.
CTRL+S	Saves the current file with the current name, location and file type.
CTRL+U	Applies or removes underlining.
CTRL+V	"Pastes" the contents of the clipboard at the current insertion point.
CTRL+X	Cuts the selected cells and places them on the clipboard.
CTRL+Z	Uses the **Undo** command to reverse the last command or cell entry.
CTRL+END	Moves to the last cell in a worksheet.
CTRL+HOME	Moves to the first cell in a worksheet.
ARROW KEYS	Move around a worksheet one cell at a time, up, down, left or right.
DELETE	Removes the contents of selected cells.
TAB	Moves one cell to the right.
SHIFT+TAB	Moves one cell to the left.
PAGE UP	Move one screen up in a worksheet.
PAGE DOWN	Move one screen down in a worksheet.
F1	Displays Microsoft Office Excel Help.
ENTER	Completes an entry in a cell or the Formula Bar and moves down one cell.

Introducing Spreadsheets

What is a Spreadsheet?

A spreadsheet is a table or grid consisting of a number of horizontal rows and vertical columns, as shown below. Microsoft Office Excel 2007 is the world's leading software for creating and editing spreadsheets. This chapter gives an overview of the sort of tasks which Excel 2007 can be used for; later chapters give step-by-step instructions on the creation of Excel spreadsheets and also charts and graphs, followed by practice exercises.

G12			f_x	=AVERAGE(B12:E12)		
	A	B	C	D	E	F	G
1							
2			Weekly Spending				
3							
4		Week1	Week2	Week3	Week4	Total	Average
5							
6	Food	£49.57	£41.21	£51.89	£49.99	£192.66	£48.17
7	Heating	£23.42	£25.48	£24.44	£28.89	£102.23	£25.56
8	Electricity	£11.33	£8.88	£9.95	£12.11	£42.27	£10.57
9	Rent	£97.00	£97.00	£97.00	£97.00	£388.00	£97.00
10	Petrol	£18.49	£17.12	£21.21	£19.82	£76.64	£19.16
11	Car	£28.00	£33.98	£49.99	£32.05	£144.02	£36.01
12	Total	£227.81	£223.67	£254.48	£239.86	£945.82	£236.46

The small boxes at the junction of each row and column are known as *cells*. A cell can contain *text*, a *number* or a *formula* to do a calculation.

Excel spreadsheets can be enormous – up to 16,384 columns and over a million rows – more than enough for managing most homes and small businesses! Cells are identified by a unique "grid reference" based on the column and row headings; in the above example, **236.46** in cell **G12** has been calculated by averaging the weekly totals in cells **B12** to **F12**.

Advantages of Spreadsheets

The difference between a spreadsheet and an ordinary table typed in a word processor is that the figures in the spreadsheet can be used for calculations and to create graphs and charts.

Spreadsheets on paper were around long before computers were invented and could involve many hours of laborious manual calculations; typical tasks would include adding up rows and columns of figures or multiplying two columns together.

Spreadsheets are ideally suited to exploit the power of a computer to do routine calculations, reducing hours of work to a matter of seconds. Not surprisingly spreadsheet programs were amongst the first applications of computers along with word processing and payroll calculations.

Excel 2007 is very easy to use

Although extremely powerful, Excel is very easy to use; even if you don't like Maths you can still make good use of the program. This is because quite complex tasks are reduced to clicking with the mouse on an icon (small picture) or on a menu option, as shown on the left. The program assumes the range of numbers you want to base the calculation on and highlights them with a dotted rectangle, as shown on the right. If necessary you can adjust the dotted rectangle by dragging with the mouse.

Σ AutoSum ▼

Σ   Sum

Average

£
36.25
45.15
17.10
9.35
=SUM(E6:E9)

Recalculation – What if?

Spreadsheet programs are widely used in business in a variety of applications. For example, in house building you could enter the costs of the materials and labour and calculate the total cost of the house. Then predict how possible alternatives would affect the total cost, such as "What if we used hardwood windows?

To find the effect of such changes on the price of the house, simply enter the new costs into the spreadsheet. The spreadsheet program automatically recalculates the new total cost of the house. This *recalculation* feature is one of the main advantages of spreadsheet programs and can save many hours of work compared with traditional methods of calculation.

Graphs and Charts

Microsoft Office Excel 2007 is also used for presenting data graphically in the form of pie charts and bar charts, etc.

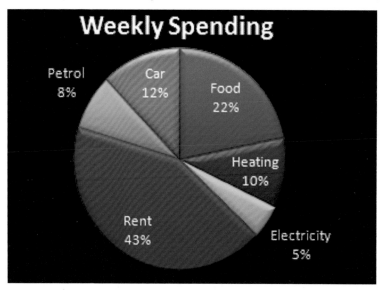

Graphs and charts enable you to compare a set of figures "at a glance". Working out the horizontal and vertical scales for a bar chart or the angles for the slices of a pie chart, is a very laborious task when done manually with pencil and paper, etc. Excel 2007 reduces the task to a few clicks with the mouse taking a matter of seconds. Charts and graphs are discussed in more detail in later chapters of this book.

Spreadsheet Applications

The next few pages give some examples of how spreadsheets can be used. In practice a spreadsheet table or worksheet might contain thousands of cells and hundreds of rows and columns. However, these small examples should give an idea of the diverse range of tasks possible with Excel 2007.

Sales of Bar Meals – Totalling Rows and Columns

The spreadsheet below involves two of the most common operations; totalling along rows and down columns. There's no need to do any mental arithmetic yourself – totalling a row or column involves only two or three clicks with a mouse. As discussed later, repeating a calculation down a column or along a row is done automatically using the *replication* facility.

G11	▼		f_x	=SUM(B11:F11)		
	A	B	C	D	E	F	G
1							
2			**Bar Meals**				
3							
4	Meal	Tues	Wed	Thurs	Fri	Sat	Total
5							
6	Pizza	3	8	9	12	17	49
7	Cod and chips	7	6	14	23	21	71
8	Scampi	2	6	8	13	18	47
9	Mushroom Risotto	3	6	5	8	12	34
10	Coq au Vin	0	8	4	7	9	28
11	Total	15	34	40	63	77	229

Cell **G11** above contains the **Total** produced by adding all the daily totals along row **11,** as shown in the Formula Bar below.

G11	▼		f_x	=SUM(B11:F11)

It's then quite easy to produce a bar chart or pie chart, etc., to show, for example, the most popular bar meals, as shown on the next page.

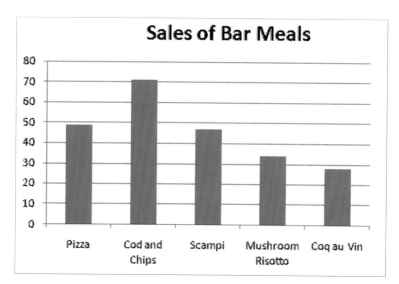

Excel 2007 does all the work for you and enables you to create a wide range of chart types in a matter of seconds.

Drink Sales – Multiplying Two Columns Together

In the example below, the sales in **£** for each type of drink is found by multiplying the price of one drink in column **C** by the **Number Sold** in Column **D**.

	E6		f_x	=C6*D6	
	A	B	C	D	E	F
1						
2			**Drink Sales**			
3						
4		Description	Price	Number Sold	Sales	
5			£		£	
6		Tea	1.25	29	36.25	
7		Coffee	1.29	35	45.15	
8		Orange	0.90	19	17.10	
9		Lemonade	0.85	11	9.35	
10			Total	94	107.85	
11						

You can see from the **Drink Sales** spreadsheet that the **Sales** figure for **Tea**, for example, in cell **E6** is **£36.25**, obtained by multiplying cell **C6** by **D6**. This is shown as **C6*D6** in the Formula Bar across the top of the **Drink Sales** worksheet.

E6	▾	f_x	=C6*D6

Calculation of Body Mass Index (BMI)

BMI is a measure of a person's weight in relation to their height. It is calculated using the following formula:

$$BMI = \frac{\text{Weight in Kilograms}}{(\text{Height in Metres}) \times (\text{Height in Metres})}$$

A spreadsheet can be used to monitor the BMI of a group of people, for example to measure the success or otherwise of a fitness program.

F9		▾	f_x	=E9/D9		
	A	B	C	D	E	F	G
1							
2			Height	Height xHeight	Weight	BMI	
3			metres		kilograms		
4							
5		Mike	1.83	3.35	108.41	32.37	
6		James	1.75	3.06	88.00	28.73	
7		Sue	1.57	2.46	52.16	21.16	
8		Jill	1.63	2.66	60.33	22.71	
9		Sarah	1.65	2.72	64.41	23.66	
10							

In the above example, the numbers in column **C** are squared i.e. multiplied by themselves, to give the numbers in column **D**. Then the **Weight** in kilograms in column **E** is divided by column **D** to give the **BMI** in column **F**.

For example, the **BMI** for **Sarah** in cell **F9** has been calculated using the formula **=E9/D9**, as shown in the Formula Bar below.

F9	▾	f_x	=E9/D9

Managing Lists of Names and Addresses

In this example no calculations are involved; Excel 2007 is being used here as a sort of database to store data.

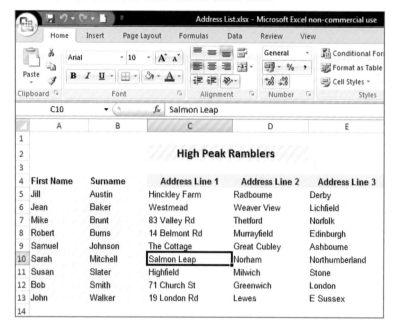

The spreadsheet is a very convenient and simple way to enter and save very large quantities of data, such as the names and addresses of customers of a business or members of a club or society. Once entered and saved, the records can be easily and quickly sorted into a particular order, such as alphabetical order of surname. You can also search for and filter out records which meet certain specified criteria.

The use of Excel 2007 as a data source for a mail merge and to print out address labels is described in detail later in this book.

Summary of Spreadsheet Advantages

- Programs like Excel 2007 are very easy to use; difficult and laborious operations are reduced to simply clicking icons and menu options.

- Excel 2007 works in an intuitive way – often anticipating correctly what you want to do.

- Spreadsheet programs save an enormous amount of time compared with manual calculations.

- A spreadsheet can be instantly sorted into alphabetical or numerical order; for example, a list of names and addresses could be sorted into surname order.

- Numerous copies can be printed out on paper quickly and easily for distribution to colleagues, etc.

- Large sheets can be presented in various stylish ready-made formats which are easy to read.

- A spreadsheet can be saved as a file on a hard disc and distributed as an e-mail attachment or on a CD.

- A spreadsheet can be edited easily and updated with the latest data from time to time. Cells produced as a result of a calculation are automatically recalculated.

- Tables of figures can be converted to attractive graphs and charts very quickly and easily, saving a great deal of time compared with traditional methods.

- An Excel spreadsheet can be imported into a Word document; for example when writing a report on sales in a business or writing up the results of an experiment.

- An Excel spreadsheet can be used to store a file of names and addresses. This can then, for example, act as the data source to print standard letters and address labels using a mail merge.

2

Introducing Excel 2007

Excel 2007 and Microsoft Office 2007

Excel 2007 is a spreadsheet program, part of the Microsoft Office 2007 suite of software. An inexpensive way to obtain Excel 2007 is to buy the Office Home and Student 2007 edition costing under £60; this software (Excel, Word and also Publisher) has been used in the production of this book. Many small businesses, students and individual users will find that the Home and Student edition of Office 2007 will meet all their requirements. All versions of Office 2007 also contain the widely used Word 2007 word processor, as shown in the table below.

	Microsoft Office Basic 2007	Microsoft Office Home & Student 2007[1]	Microsoft Office Standard 2007	Microsoft Office Small Business 2007	Microsoft Office Professional 2007	Microsoft Office Ultimate 2007 NEW!
Microsoft Office Word 2007	●	●	●	●	●	●
Microsoft Office Excel 2007	●	●	●	●	●	●
Microsoft Office PowerPoint 2007		●	●	●	●	●
Microsoft Office Outlook 2007	●		●			
Microsoft Office Outlook 2007 with Business Contact Manager				●	●	●
Microsoft Office Publisher 2007				●	●	●
Microsoft Office Access 2007					●	●

In order to use Office 2007 and Excel 2007 you need a computer equipped with either Windows XP or Windows Vista. Excel 2007 introduces a new "user interface" in the form of a *tabbed Ribbon*, discussed shortly, but apart from that much of the material in this book also applies to spreadsheets in general, including earlier versions of Excel.

Installing Excel 2007

As mentioned earlier, one of the most popular ways to get Excel 2007 up and running on your computer is to install the Office Home and Student 2007 edition. The package consists of a plastic box containing the software on a single CD. There should be a label on the top of the box indicating that the copy of the software is genuine. There is also a list of minimum hardware and software requirements needed to run the software, namely:

500MHz or faster processor

256MB RAM

1.5MB available hard disc space

CD-ROM or DVD drive

1028x768 or higher resolution monitor

Windows Vista or XP with Service Pack 2

If your computer was bought within the last few years it should comfortably meet these requirements.

Multiple Installations from a Single Office CD

Recognising that many homes now have more than one computer, one Office Home and Student 2007 CD may be legally installed on up to 3 computers.

The Product Key

On the back of an inner plastic case in the Office package is the PRODUCT KEY label. This is your licence to install the software – without it you can't validate and activate the software. It's worth making a copy of the 25-character key and storing it in a safe place. You might have a technical problem later and need the key to re-install the Office software.

At the bottom of a legally-obtained CD is a hologram in which the word **GENUINE** alternates with the word **MICROSOFT**. Users of illegal copies of software may find they can't install the latest software upgrades or get telephone support.

During the installation process you will be asked to enter your 25-character product key – letters must be in upper case. If you don't enter a product key you will only be able to use the software for a limited time, e.g. 30 days.

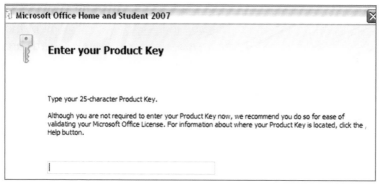

If the product key is genuine, a green tick appears and you then click **Continue** to carry on with the installation. After choosing to either **Upgrade** or **Customize** you are presented with a window showing the **Progress** of the installation as a percentage. Finally you are informed that the software has been successfully installed and you can, if you wish, click **Go to Office Online** to get updates, help and online services.

As with many software installations, you need to restart the computer before using the software for the first time.

Activation

Microsoft Office has to be *activated*, a process intended to prevent single-user editions of software being installed on more than one computer. (Office Home & Student 2007 is an exception, being licensed for up to 3 installations). During the installation process you are given the choice to activate over the Internet or by telephone. If you don't activate your copy of Office you will only be able to use the software for a limited time.

Launching Excel 2007 from the All Programs Menu

At the end of the installation process you will find entries for **Microsoft Office**, including **Excel 2007**, in the **All Programs** menu accessed via the **Start** orb in the bottom left-hand corner of the screen, as shown below.

Excel 2007 can now be launched by clicking its entry in the **All Programs** menu shown above. As shown on later pages, a new, radically different, "user interface" has been introduced in Microsoft Office 2007. This has been applied to the Excel, Word and PowerPoint 2007 programs; having so many features in common makes the programs easier to learn and use.

Launching Excel 2007 from the Start Menu

After you have used Excel 2007 for the first time, you don't need to go onto the **All Programs** menu shown on the previous page. Using Excel 2007 the first time places an entry for the program directly on the **Start** menu as shown below.

A single click on the Excel 2007 entry above launches the program.

Launching Excel 2007 from an Icon on the Desktop

Right-click over the entry for **Microsoft Office Excel 2007** in the **All Programs** or **Start** menus shown previously. Then click **Send To** from the menu which appears and select **Desktop (create shortcut)** as shown below.

An icon for Excel 2007 will now be part of your Windows Desktop, as shown on the right. Double click this icon every time you want to launch Excel 2007 and start a new spreadsheet session.

The Excel 2007 Screen

When you launch Excel 2007 using one of the methods just described you will see a blank worksheet ready for you to start entering headings, data and formulae, discussed in detail shortly.

The Excel 2007 Ribbon

Along the top of the screen is the *tabbed Ribbon*, a new feature introduced in Office 2007. A section of the tabbed Ribbon is shown below, with tabs such as **Home**, I**nsert** and **Page Layout**.

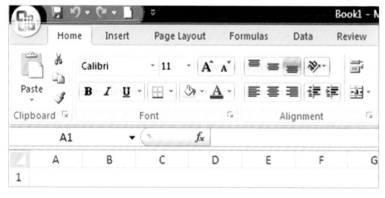

When you select a different tab, such as **Page Layout** above, the Ribbon changes to display a different set of icons or tools. The tools displayed on the Ribbon may also change automatically when you select a different task, such as a chart.

The Office Button

A worksheet is created, saved, edited, printed and formatted using various tabs and icons on the Excel Ribbon, such as **Home**, **Insert**, **Page Layout**, etc., shown on the previous screen extract. The **Office Button** on the left of the Ribbon opens the menu shown on the right, with options to **Save** and **Print** a worksheet.

If you are connected to the Internet, click the **Office Button** to display the menu shown on the right and then press the **F1** key located near the top left of your keyboard. The **Microsoft Office Online Help** appears, open at the **Excel** section, as shown in the extract below. There is also a **Search** facility to find help on particular topics.

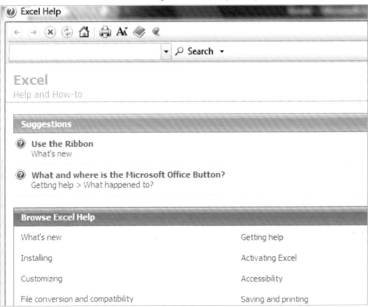

The Home Tab

Each tab on the Ribbon is divided into a number of groups, so that for example, the **Home** tab has groups such as **Clipboard**, **Font** and **Alignment** shown below. These include many tools for formatting the text and data in the cells, similar to those found in a word processor.

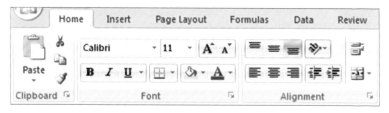

On the left of the **Home** tab on the Ribbon is the **Clipboard** group, shown on the left, with icons to **Cut**, **Copy** and **Paste** data between worksheets or into a word processor document, for example.

The **Format Painter** on the right provides a quick way of copying the formatting of one piece of text or numbers to another; this includes the text size, bold, italics, font colour, or numbers in currency format, for example.

Further along the **Home** tab on the Ribbon there are groups called **Number**, **Styles**, **Cells** and **Editing**. These provide tools for formatting numbers and text in cells and inserting and deleting cells and entire rows and columns.

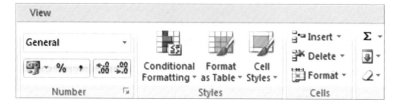

The Insert Tab

The **Insert** tab on the Ribbon, shown below, allows various features to be inserted into a worksheet. These include many different types of graphs and charts, such as **Column**, **Line**, **Pie** and **Bar Charts** as shown on the **Charts** group on the **Insert** tab shown below.

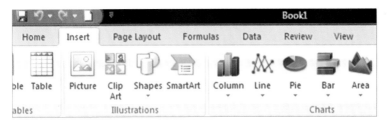

The Formulas Tab

The **Formulas** tab shown in the screen extract below contains tools to perform a very wide range of mathematical calculations; most users will, however, find their work is mainly confined to common operations such as addition, subtraction, multiplication, division and averages.

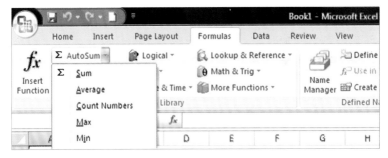

The many icons representing tools on the various tabs on the Ribbon provide a quick and easy way to create, format and edit a spreadsheet.

The Excel Ribbon and tabs are discussed further in the context of the worked examples which follow in the rest of this book.

Worksheets and Workbooks

In Excel 2007 a spreadsheet is also referred to as a *worksheet*. Several related worksheets can be saved as a single file known as a *workbook*. You can move between different worksheets by clicking the tabs, **Sheet1**, **Sheet2**, **Sheet3**, etc., at the bottom of the screen.

When you save your work, all of the worksheets are saved in one workbook, as a single file on your hard disc. If you don't give the new workbook a name it's saved by default as **Book1** or **Book2**, etc. The icon on the left and on the right above allows you to insert an extra worksheet in the workbook.

Changing the View on a Worksheet

At the bottom of the Excel 2007 screen there is a scroll bar allowing you to pan across a worksheet. There is also a slider allowing you to alter the **Zoom** to enlarge or reduce the view.

In the extract below the **Zoom** slider has been set at nearly 300%

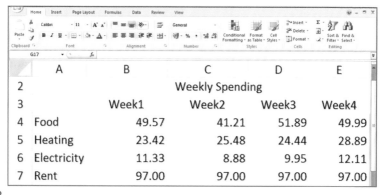

	A	B	C	D	E
2			Weekly Spending		
3		Week1	Week2	Week3	Week4
4	Food	49.57	41.21	51.89	49.99
5	Heating	23.42	25.48	24.44	28.89
6	Electricity	11.33	8.88	9.95	12.11
7	Rent	97.00	97.00	97.00	97.00

3

Entering Labels, Numbers and Formulas

Moving Around in a Worksheet

After you launch Excel 2007 from the Start menu or by double-clicking a desktop icon, as described in the previous chapter, you are presented with a new sheet consisting of a blank grid of cells. Click anywhere on the worksheet, such as cell **D3** shown below, and you are ready to start entering data.

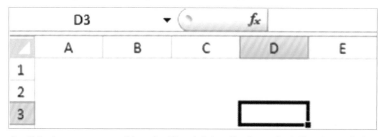

As this is a new workbook, **Book1** is displayed at the top of the screen until you save the spreadsheet with a suitable name, which you make up. There are tabs for **Sheet1**,

Book1 - Microsoft Excel

Sheet2, **Sheet3**, etc., along the bottom of the worksheet, as shown below.

Moving Down a Column

Now try pressing the **Return** or **Enter** key repeatedly; the cursor moves down the current column from cell to cell. You'll soon find the row numbers going into the hundreds, as in cell **D244** below.

Moving Along a Row

From the current cell, press the **Tab** key shown on the right. This moves the cursor along a row from *left to right*.

Tab

Holding down the **Shift** key while pressing the **Tab** key moves the cursor along a row from *right to left*.

Shift

Alternatively the four arrow or cursor keys, shown on the left, allow the cursor to be moved around the worksheet in any direction.

On large worksheets the horizontal and vertical scroll bars can be used to move to a certain part of the sheet.

The **Page Up** and **Page Down** keys move up and down the spreadsheet in steps of 25 rows at a time.

To move quickly to the beginning or end of a spreadsheet, use the key combinations **Ctrl+Home** or **Ctrl+End** respectively. (While holding down the **Ctrl** key, press the **Home** or **End** key).

Moving to a Specified Cell

Click in the Formula Bar at the top of the worksheet, delete the current cell reference and enter the one you wish to move to, e.g. **D273**. When you press **Enter** the cursor is placed in the required cell.

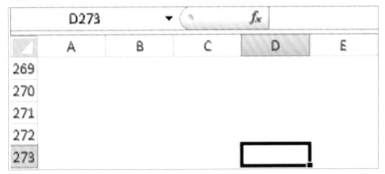

Cell Contents

In the **Drink Sales** spreadsheet below, the currently selected cell **D10** is shown in the Formula Bar across the top of the worksheet. Also displayed are the cell contents, in this case the formula **=D6+D7+D8+D9.**

D10	▼	f_x	=D6+D7+D8+D9	
	A	B	C	D	E
1					
2			**Drink Sales**		
3					
4		Description	Price	Number Sold	Sales
5			£		£
6		Tea	1.25	29	36.25
7		Coffee	1.29	35	45.15
8		Orange	0.90	19	17.1
9		Lemonade	0.85	11	9.35
10			Total	94	107.85

Entering Labels into a Cell

In the above small spreadsheet or worksheet, you can see that some cells contain words or *labels*, such as the worksheet title **Drink Sales** and the column and row headings, e.g. **Description**, **Price**, etc. To enter a label, simply click in the required cell and start typing. When you've finished typing, press **Enter** or use one of the other methods described earlier to move to the next cell. Labels can be edited at any time, after double-clicking in the appropriate cell.

Widening a Column to Accommodate Labels or Data, etc.

If a column is not wide enough for a label, data, or formula, place the cursor on the vertical line to the right of the letter at the top of the column. A small cross appears. This is used for adjusting the width of a column, as shown on the next page.

In the example below, to widen Column **D**, drag the cross shown on the right of the header for Column **D**. Column **D** can also be widened by dragging the cross which appears between Columns **C** and **D**, although this reduces the width of Column **C**.

Entering Numbers into a Cell

Click in the cell and type the numbers straight in. You can format the numbers later, e.g. to display every number with two decimal places or in *integer* format (no figures after the decimal point). Formatting numbers including the **£** sign in the **Currency** format is discussed in more detail later in this book.

Entering a Formula into a Cell

First select the cell where the answer is to appear. Then the formula is either typed into this cell or entered by selecting a function, such as **Average**, for example, from the **Formulas** tab on the Excel 2007 Ribbon.

=D6+D7+D8+D9	Add together the contents of cells **D6** to **D9**.
=D10-D8	Subtract the contents of cell **D8** from **D10**.
=C6*D6	Multiply contents of cell **C6** by contents of **D6**.
=E10/D10	Divide contents of cell **E10** by **D10**.

Please note:

> * is used as the spreadsheet multiplication sign.
>
> / is the sign for division.

While you are typing a formula, it is displayed both in the cell and in the Formula Bar near the top of the spreadsheet

| | × ✓ f_x | =D6+D7+D8+D9 |

When the formula has been correctly entered, click the tick in the Formula Bar shown above, or press **Enter**. Once the calculation is complete a calculated cell, such as **D10** in the worksheet below, does not normally display the formula, in this case **=D6+D7+D8+D9**.

D10	▼		f_x	=D6+D7+D8+D9	
	A	B	C	D	E
1					
2			**Drink Sales**		
3					
4		Description	Price	Number Sold	Sales
5			£		£
6		Tea	1.25	29	36.25
7		Coffee	1.29	35	45.15
8		Orange	0.90	19	17.1
9		Lemonade	0.85	11	9.35
10			Total	94	107.85

Only the answer to the sum appears in the cell **D10** above, even though the formula was originally entered in this calculated cell.

Displaying the Formula in a Calculated Cell

To display a formula in a particular calculated cell, double-click in the cell, as shown below for cell **D10** of the **Drink Sales** worksheet. The formula **=D6+D7+D8+D9** then appears, as shown below, instead of the answer **94** as shown above.

Lemonade	0.85	11	9.35
	Total	=D6+D7+D8+D9	107.85

Totalling Rows and Columns – the SUM Function

In the previous example, a column containing 4 numbers was totalled using the formula **=D6+D7+D8+D9**. In a business spreadsheet it may be necessary to total hundreds of numbers down a column or along a row. For this task, Excel 2007 provides the **SUM** function which can be manually typed e.g.

=SUM(D6:D9)

In this example, **(D6:D9)** refers to the *range* of cells from **D6** to **D9** inclusive. To save typing in by hand this frequently-used function, Excel 2007 provides the **AutoSum** icon on the **Formulas** tab on the Ribbon, shown below.

If you select a cell then click the **AutoSum** icon, Excel assumes you want to add up the numbers above or to the left of the currently selected cell. The assumed range is shown dotted in the example on the right. It's a good idea to check that the range of cells which Excel has assumed is correct. If necessary, manually alter the range by editing in the cell or in the **Formula Bar** as shown below.

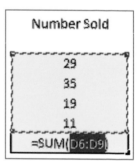

When you are satisfied the formula is correct either press **Enter** or click the tick in the Formula Bar as shown above, to complete the calculation. To redo the calculation from scratch, click the cross in the Formula Bar.

Multiplying Two Cells Together

In the **Drink Sales** spreadsheet shown on page 23, the value of the **Sales** of each drink in Column **E** is calculated by multiplying the **Price** in Column **C** by the **Number** sold in Column **D**.

This is achieved for **Tea**, for example, by entering the formula **=C6*D6** in cell **E6**, as shown below.

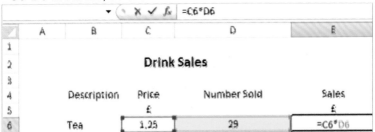

When you press **Enter** or click the tick in the Formula Bar shown above, the answer **36.25** appears in cell **E6,** shown below.

	Description	Price £	Number Sold	Sales £
4				
5				
6	Tea	1.25	29	36.25

Now the formulas for the **Sales** in £ for **Coffee**, **Orange** and **Lemonade** must be calculated and the answers placed in cells **E7** to **E9**. This could be done by typing the formula into each cell in Column **E**, as shown below under **Sales**.

	Description	Price £	Number Sold	Sales £
4				
5				
6	Tea	1.25	29	=C6*D6
7	Coffee	1.29	35	=C7*D7
8	Orange	0.9	19	=C8*D8
9	Lemonade	0.85	11	=C9*D9

This would take too long on a large spreadsheet and the *replication* feature is provided to enable a formula to be copied easily and quickly by dragging with the mouse, as discussed in the next chapter. Cell references are adjusted automatically.

Editing a Cell at a Later Date

You can edit a cell containing a label, number or formula at any time in the future. The cell contents can be edited either in the cell or in the Formula Bar (sometimes also called the Entry Bar).

- To edit the cell contents by typing in the cell, *double-click* in the cell and start editing.

- To edit the cell contents by typing in the Formula Bar, click once in the required cell then click in the Formula Bar and start editing.

Functions

For more complex calculations, a complete set of mathematical *functions* is available by clicking **Insert Function** on the **Formulas** group on the Excel 2007 Ribbon, as shown below.

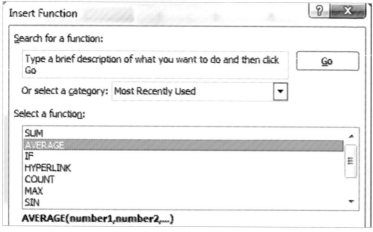

You can also search for a suitable function by entering a description of what you want to do. Many users will probably find the basic mathematical operations of addition, subtraction, multiplication, division and averages are more than adequate in most applications of spreadsheets.

4

Creating, Saving and Printing a Spreadsheet

This chapter takes you through the following spreadsheet skills:

- Starting a new spreadsheet
- Entering text and numbers
- Totalling rows and columns, including replication
- Saving and printing the spreadsheet
- Displaying and printing formulas

The next few pages describe the entry and calculation of the **Weekly Spending** spreadsheet shown below. You may wish to read through these notes first then attempt the practice exercise at the end of this chapter.

G10			f_x	=AVERAGE(B10:E10)		
A	B	C	D	E	F	G
1						
2		Weekly Spending				
3		Week1	Week2	Week3	Week4	Total	Average
4 Food	49.57	41.21	51.89	49.99	192.66	48.17
5 Heating	23.42	25.48	24.44	28.89	102.23	25.56
6 Electricity	11.33	8.88	9.95	12.11	42.27	10.57
7 Rent	97.00	97.00	97.00	97.00	388.00	97.00
8 Petrol	18.49	17.12	21.21	19.82	76.64	19.16
9 Car	28.00	33.98	49.99	32.05	144.02	36.01
10 Total	227.81	223.67	254.48	239.86	945.82	236.46

Excel 2007 must first be launched from the **Start** or **All Programs** menus or by clicking on the icon on the desktop as discussed in Chapter 2. You are then presented with a blank worksheet in which to start typing the labels, data and formulas.

Entering the Labels and Headings

Referring to the spreadsheet on the previous page, first the title **Weekly Spending** is entered. Then the column and row headings or labels **Week1**, **Week2**, etc., **Food**, **Heating**, etc., can be entered. (Widening a column to accommodate a wide label is described on page 21).

	A	B	C	D	E
	B10	▼		f_x	
1					
2			Weekly Spending		
3		Week1	Week2	Week3	Week4
4	Food	49.57	41.21	51.89	49.99
5	Heating	23.42	25.48	24.44	28.89
6	Electricity	11.33	8.88	9.95	12.11
7	Rent	97.00	97.00	97.00	97.00
8	Petrol	18.49	17.12	21.21	19.82
9	Car	28.00	33.98	49.99	32.05
10	Total				

Entering the Numbers

The numbers are typed straight into the cells. A convenient method is to work down the columns, pressing **Enter** to move down to the next cell. *Formatting* the numbers, for example in the **Currency** format with a £ sign and two places after the decimal point, is discussed in Chapter 5.

Calculated Cells – Totalling a Column

A formula must be entered in cell **B10** to calculate the **Total** expenditure in **Week1**.

To do this, click in cell **B10** then click the **AutoSum** icon shown on the right. This is found on the Excel 2007 Ribbon with the **Formulas** tab selected.

	Σ AutoSum ▾

| SUM | ▾ | ✕ ✓ f_x | =SUM(B4:B9) |

	A	B	C	D	E
1					
2			Weekly Spending		
3		Week1	Week2	Week3	Week4
4	Food	49.57	41.21	51.89	49.99
5	Heating	23.42	25.48	24.44	28.89
6	Electricity	11.33	8.88	9.95	12.11
7	Rent	97.00	97.00	97.00	97.00
8	Petrol	18.49	17.12	21.21	19.82
9	Car	28.00	33.98	49.99	32.05
10	Total	=SUM(B4:B9)			

If you are happy that the formula and the range of cells within the dotted rectangle are correct, click the tick in the Formula Bar to carry out the calculation.

| SUM | ▾ | ✕ ✓ f_x | =SUM(B4:B9) |

If the formula is not correct, click the cross and type the correct formula in the Formula Bar or adjust the range of cells by dragging the dotted rectangle, using the mouse. When the calculation of the **Total** is complete, the answer **227.81**, not the formula, is displayed in cell **B10** as shown on the right.

8	Petrol	18.49
9	Car	28.00
10	Total	227.81

Replication

This is a great labour-saving feature of spreadsheets. Having calculated the total for **Week1**, the same method can be applied to **Week2**, **Week3** and **Week4** by a simple mouse operation.

The method of replication is as follows:

1.   Select the cell containing the formula to be replicated, cell **B10** in this example.

2.   Allow the cursor to hover over the bottom right-hand corner of the cell until a small cross appears, as shown below to the right of **227.81**.

8	Petrol	18.49	17.12	21.21	19.82
9	Car	28.00	33.98	49.99	32.05
10	Total	227.81			
11					

3.   Hold down the left mouse button and drag the cross over the cells where the calculation is to be replicated. The totals for **Week2**, **Week3** and **Week4** (**223.67**, **254.48** and **239.86**) appear in the cells automatically as shown below.

8	Petrol	18.49	17.12	21.21	19.82
9	Car	28.00	33.98	49.99	32.05
10	Total	227.81	223.67	254.48	239.86

Displaying the Formulas in All Calculated Cells

Select the **Formulas** tab on the Excel 2007 Ribbon and then click **Show Formulas** on the right of the tab. All of the formulas replicated along row 10 of the **Weekly Spending** spreadsheet are then displayed, as shown below.

Show Formulas

9	Car	28.00	33.98	49.99	32.05
10	Total	=SUM(B4:B9)	=SUM(C4:C9)	=SUM(D4:D9)	=SUM(E4:E9)

Totalling Along a Row

Returning to the **Weekly Spending** spreadsheet, we might wish to calculate the amount spent on each item — **Food**, **Heating**, **Electricity**, etc., over the 4-week period. This involves totalling along each horizontal row of the worksheet in turn.

First the label **Total** is entered in cell **F3**. Then the formula to total along the **Food** row, **=SUM(B4:E4)** is entered in cell **F4**. This can be entered either by typing the formula into the cell or by clicking the **AutoSum** icon on **Formulas** tab on the Excel 2007 Ribbon.

Σ AutoSum ▾

	SUM		▾	X ✓ ƒx	=SUM(B4:E4)
	A	B	C	D	E	F
1						
2			Weekly Spending			
3		Week1	Week2	Week3	Week4	Total
4	Food	49.57	41.21	51.89	49.99	=SUM(B4:E4
5	Heating	23.42	25.48	24.44	28.89	
6	Electricity	11.33	8.88	9.95	12.11	
7	Rent	97.00	97.00	97.00	97.00	
8	Petrol	18.49	17.12	21.21	19.82	
9	Car	28.00	33.98	49.99	32.05	
10	Total	227.81	223.67	254.48	239.86	

AutoSum has a guess at the range of cells you want to total, as shown above by the dotted rectangle. In some situations this assumed range may not be what you intend, depending on the particular context, so check the range carefully. Then click the tick in the Formula Bar or press **Enter** if you are satisfied with the formula. Otherwise click the cross and redo the calculation.

SUM   ▾   X ✓ ƒx =SUM(B4:E4)

Replicating a Formula Down a Column

We now need to repeat the row totalling for the other items of expenditure, **Heating**, **Electricity**, **Rent**, etc. This means copying the formula in cell **F4**, but making the necessary adjustments to the cell references, i.e. **=SUM(B5:E5)**, **=SUM(B6:E6)**, etc.

First click in cell **F4** and allow the cursor to hover over the bottom right of the cell until a small cross appears. Keeping the left mouse button held down, drag the cross down the column, over the cells into which the formula is to be replicated.

After you release the mouse button the answers to the row totals appear in the cells, as shown below.

	E	F
	Week4	Total
	49.99	192.66
	28.89	
	12.11	
	97.00	
	19.82	
	32.05	
	239.86	

F10			f_x =SUM(B10:E10)			
	A	B	C	D	E	F
1						
2			Weekly Spending			
3		Week1	Week2	Week3	Week4	Total
4	Food	49.57	41.21	51.89	49.99	192.66
5	Heating	23.42	25.48	24.44	28.89	102.23
6	Electricity	11.33	8.88	9.95	12.11	42.27
7	Rent	97.00	97.00	97.00	97.00	388.00
8	Petrol	18.49	17.12	21.21	19.82	76.64
9	Car	28.00	33.98	49.99	32.05	144.02
10	Total	227.81	223.67	254.48	239.86	945.82

Click **Show Formulas** on the **Formulas** tab on the Ribbon to display the formulas replicated from cell **F4** to cells **F5** to **F10**, as shown in the extract on the right.

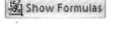

Total
=SUM(B4:E4)
=SUM(B5:E5)
=SUM(B6:E6)
=SUM(B7:E7)
=SUM(B8:E8)
=SUM(B9:E9)
=SUM(B10:E10)

Using the Average Function

To find the average amount spent on each item, (**Food**, **Heating**, etc.), first place a label, **Average**, in cell **G3**. Then place the cursor in cell **G4** and click the small downward pointing arrow next to **AutoSum** on the Excel 2007 Ribbon.

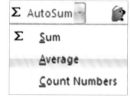

Now click **Average** shown above on the right and you are presented with the average calculation shown below.

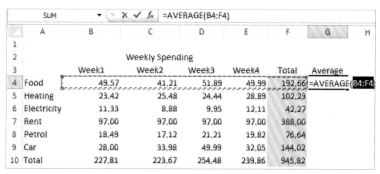

In this case the range of numbers, **(B4:F4)**, assumed for the average, is incorrect. This is because the **Total** of **192.66** in **F4** has been wrongly included along with the weekly spending figures in **B4** to **E4**. We can correct this by clicking in the formula bar shown below and editing the formula to show **=Average (B4:E4)**.

▼	X	✓	*fx*	=AVERAGE(B4:E4)

When you are happy with the formula click the tick and the first (correct) **Average**, **48.17**, should appear in cell **G4**. Now replicate the formula down column **G** by dragging the cross, as previously described, to complete the **Average** column, as shown on the right.

Total	Average
192.66	48.17
102.23	25.56
42.27	10.57
388.00	97.00
76.64	19.16
144.02	36.01
945.82	236.46

Saving a Spreadsheet

After you have created a spreadsheet it needs to be saved on your hard disc. Then it can be retrieved at a later date and edited or extended. With a large spreadsheet containing important data it's essential to make a backup copy on a removable storage medium such as a CD or a memory stick and this is discussed later in Chapter 9, Safety Precautions.

To save a spreadsheet as a file on your hard disc, click the **Office Button** on the Excel 2007 Ribbon to open the menu shown on the right. Now click **Save As** from the menu to open the **Save As** dialogue box shown below. (You don't need to wait until the spreadsheet is complete before saving it. You can save the initial blank sheet using **Save As** and a made-up name. Then in future regularly click the disc icon on the Excel Ribbon to keep saving the latest version of the sheet.)

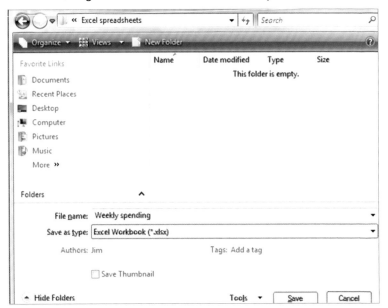

At the top of the **Save As** dialogue box shown on the previous page, is the *folder*, called **Excel spreadsheets** in this example. This is the location on your hard disc where the file will be saved. You can change to another folder by browsing through the **Favorite Links** such as **Computer**, shown on the left of the **Save As** dialogue box on the previous page. Alternatively you can click **New Folder** shown below and create and name your own folder such as **Excel spreadsheets**.

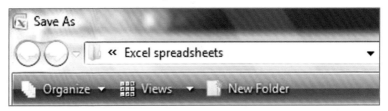

At the bottom of the **Save As** dialogue box shown on the previous page, you can enter a name for your spreadsheet. Excel 2007 calls them *Workbooks* and *Worksheets* and by default calls new workbooks **Book1**, **Book2**, etc. Delete the default file name **Book1.xlsx** and type in a suitable name such as **Weekly spending** as shown below.

File name:	Weekly spending
Save as type:	Excel Workbook (*.xlsx)

Make sure the **Save as type** is set at **Excel Workbook(*.xlsx)** as shown above and click the **Save** button at the bottom right of the **Save As** dialogue box. The file name extension **.xlsx** is added automatically.

Now you've given the spreadsheet a name and specified a folder location, all subsequent saves can be done by simply clicking the disc icon shown on the right. This is located above the Ribbon, next to the **Office Button**, as shown on the left.

Printing a Spreadsheet

You may want to print a "hard copy" of a spreadsheet so that it can be viewed away from the computer. Click the **Office Button** and then select **Print** and you are presented with three options:

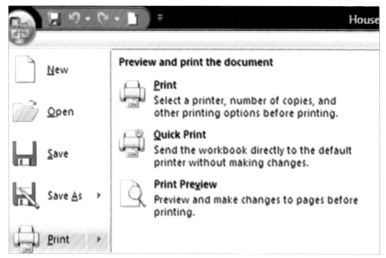

Print and **Quick Print** make a copy on paper, but it may not be in the best format. **Print** allows you to specify the number of copies and also to print selected cells or an entire workbook consisting of several worksheets (spreadsheets). **Print Preview** allows you to see what the printed sheet will look like on the page and make adjustments before committing it to paper.

Portrait or Landscape

A spreadsheet is often too wide to fit on a single sheet of paper, such as A4. A wider sheet can be printed by setting the sheet in **Landscape** orientation, (paper sideways) rather than **Portrait** (paper upright). This option can be set by clicking **Orientation** on the **Page Layout** tab of the Excel 2007 Ribbon.

Printing Gridlines

The gridlines marking the rows and columns can be printed on paper by selecting the **Page Layout** tab on the Excel 2007 Ribbon, then making sure there is a tick next to **Print** under **Gridlines** in the **Sheet Options** group, as shown on the right.

Displaying and Printing Formulas

To print a copy of a spreadsheet showing all of the formulas used, select the **Formulas** tab on the Excel 2007 Ribbon,

then click **Show Formulas**. The calculated cells now display the formulas, not the answers. However, when the formulas are displayed the column widths are greatly increased. These can be reduced substantially by dragging, as discussed in Chapter 3. It may also be advantageous to set the spreadsheet in **Landscape** orientation as described on the previous page. An extract from the **Weekly Spending** spreadsheet with the formulas displayed is shown below. The spreadsheet and the formulas can now be printed on paper in the usual way.

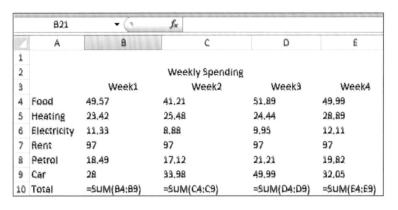

	A	B	C	D	E
1					
2			Weekly Spending		
3		Week1	Week2	Week3	Week4
4	Food	49.57	41.21	51.89	49.99
5	Heating	23.42	25.48	24.44	28.89
6	Electricity	11.33	8.88	9.95	12.11
7	Rent	97	97	97	97
8	Petrol	18.49	17.12	21.21	19.82
9	Car	28	33.98	49.99	32.05
10	Total	=SUM(B4:B9)	=SUM(C4:C9)	=SUM(D4:D9)	=SUM(E4:E9)

Exercise 1: Creating a Spreadsheet and Entering Data and Formulas

1. Launch Excel 2007.

2. Enter the title **Weekly Spending**.

3. On a row below the title, enter the column headings **Week1**, **Week2**, **Week3**, **Week4**. You may wish to align the column headings using one of the icons in the **Alignment** group on the **Home** tab of the Ribbon. First select the entire row by clicking in the box containing the row number.

4. Enter in the first column the following row labels, which can be left-aligned after clicking in the column header box at the top of the spreadsheet:

   Food, **Heating**, **Electricity**, **Rent**, **Petrol**, **Car**, **Total**

5. Enter the following numeric data:

	Week1	Week2	Week3	Week4
Food	49.57	41.21	51.89	49.99
Heating	23.42	25.48	24.44	28.89
Electricity	11.33	8.88	9.95	12.11
Rent	97.00	97.00	97.00	97.00
Petrol	18.49	17.12	21.21	19.82
Car	28.00	33.98	49.99	32.05

6. Enter a formula to calculate the **Total** spending for **Week1**.

7. Replicate this formula for the other weekly totals.

8. Save the spreadsheet with a name such as **Spending1**.

9. Print a copy of the spreadsheet on paper.

10. Display all the formulas on the screen and print a copy.

5

Editing and Formatting

This chapter covers the following spreadsheet skills:

- Altering the cell contents – numbers, labels or formulas
- Deleting rows and columns
- Inserting rows and columns
- Formatting text – font style, size, colour, alignment
- Formatting numbers – whole numbers, decimal places, currency format, etc.

Editing the Cell Contents

The method of editing a cell is basically the same whether the cell contains text (labels, headings, etc.), numbers or a formula.

The contents of a cell can be edited either by typing the amendment in the cell itself or by typing in the Formula Bar above the spreadsheet.

Editing in the Cell

To edit the cell contents in the cell, double-click in the cell; the cursor flashes in the cell allowing you to type in the new contents. Press **Enter** to complete the amendment.

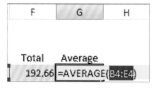

Editing in the Formula Bar

Click once in the required cell then click again in the Formula Bar. Now type the amendment in the Formula Bar then click the tick to complete the new entry.

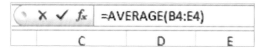

Deleting a Row

It may be necessary to delete a row from a spreadsheet; for example, to remove the **Petrol** row from the **Weekly Spending** spreadsheet shown below.

Select or highlight the row by clicking in the box on the extreme left of the row, in this example the box containing the row number **8** next to the label **Petrol,** as shown below:

	A	B	C	D
			f_x	Petrol
A8	▼			
1				
2			Weekly Spending	
3		Week1	Week2	Week3
4	Food	49.57	41.21	51.89
5	Heating	23.42	25.48	24.44
6	Electricity	11.33	8.88	9.95
7	Rent	97.00	97.00	97.00
8	Petrol	18.49	17.12	21.21
9	Car	28.00	33.98	49.99

Now click the small arrow to the right of **Delete** in the **Cells** group on the **Home** tab as shown below. Then select **Delete Sheet Rows**. All of the cell contents are removed and the space previously taken by the row is closed up, i.e. no blank row is left.

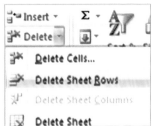

You can also delete a row by selecting the row then pressing the **Delete** key. This removes the cell contents but a blank row remains.

Deleting a Column

Highlight the column by clicking in the column header, i.e. the box containing the column reference – **C** in the example below.

	A	B	C	D
1				
2			Weekly Spending	
3		Week1	Week2	Week3
4	Food	49.57	41.21	51.89
5	Heating	23.42	25.48	24.44
6	Electricity	11.33	8.88	9.95
7	Rent	97.00	97.00	97.00
8	Petrol	18.49	17.12	21.21

Now click the small arrow next to **Delete** in the **Cells** group on the **Home** tab. Then select **Delete Sheet Columns** as shown on the right. This removes the entire column. The space previously taken by the column is closed up so that no blank column remains.

You can also delete a column by selecting the column then pressing the **Delete** key. This removes the cell contents but a blank column remains.

Recovering from Mistakes – the Undo Feature

If you make a mistake with any operation such as deleting cells, the situation can be recovered by clicking the **Undo** icon shown on the right. This is found on the **Quick Access Toolbar** above the Excel Ribbon, shown below.

Inserting a New Row

Click anywhere in the row which is to be immediately *below* the new row. In the above example, the cursor was placed in the row for **Electricity**.

	A	B	C	D	E
	E6			f_x	
1					
2			Weekly Spending		
3		Week1	Week2	Week3	Week4
4	Food	49.57	41.21	51.89	49.99
5	Heating	23.42	25.48	24.44	28.89
6					
7	Electricity	11.33	8.88	9.95	12.11
8	Rent	97.00	97.00	97.00	97.00
9	Petrol	18.49	17.12	21.21	19.82
10	Car	28.00	33.98	49.99	32.05
11	Total	227.81	223.67	254.48	239.86

Then click the arrow to the right of **Insert** on the **Cells** group on the Ribbon. Now click **Insert Sheet Rows** as shown on the right. A new, blank row is inserted ready for you to start entering the data.

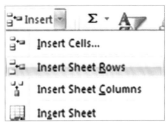

Notice that the formulas for the totals are now in row **11** and not **10**. Excel 2007 automatically takes account of this and changes the formulas accordingly. For example, the original **Total** in cell **B10** above was **=SUM(B4:B9)**. After inserting a new row, the **Total**, now in cell **B11**, becomes **=SUM(B4:B10)**. The other totals along row **11** are adjusted automatically in a similar way as shown below.

10	Car	28	33.98	49.99
11	Total	=SUM(B4:B10)	=SUM(C4:C10)	=SUM(D4:D10)

Inserting a New Column

Click anywhere in the column which is to be to the *right* of the new column. In the example below, the cursor was placed in the column for **Week3**, originally Column **D**.

	A	B	C	D	E	F
1						
2			Weekly Spending			
3		Week1	Week2		Week3	Week4
4	Food	49.57	41.21		51.89	49.99
5	Heating	23.42	25.48		24.44	28.89
6	Electricity	11.33	8.88		9.95	12.11
7	Rent	97.00	97.00		97.00	97.00
8	Petrol	18.49	17.12		21.21	19.82
9	Car	28.00	33.98		49.99	32.05
10	Total	227.81	223.67		254.48	239.86

Then click the arrow to the right of **Insert** in the **Cells** group on the Ribbon. Next select **Insert Sheet Columns** as shown on the right. A new blank column is inserted as shown above, ready for the new data to be entered.

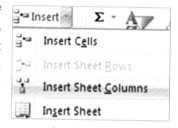

Insert

Insert Cells
Insert Sheet Rows
Insert Sheet Columns
Insert Sheet

Please Note:

Excel 2007 adjusts formulas in calculated cells automatically when rows and columns are inserted or deleted. However, it's a good idea to display each formula and quickly check that cell ranges such as **(B4:F4)**, for example, are correct.

As discussed earlier, formulas are displayed in the Formula Bar at the top of a worksheet or displayed in a calculated cell by double-clicking in the cell. Alternatively click **Show Formulas** on the **Formulas** tab on the Excel 2007 Ribbon. Windows Vista users may need to close the Windows Sidebar to display the **Show Formulas** icon in full.

Exercise 2: Editing a Spreadsheet

This exercise covers the editing skills described in the previous section. Please refer back to the notes if you need help with any of the tasks.

1. Load up the spreadsheet saved in Exercise 1 on page 38, which you may have saved with the suggested title **Spending1**.

2. Please make the following amendments: The cost of **Heating** in **Week1** should be **28.59**. The amount spent on **Rent** in **Week4** should have been **109.00**. (Omit the **£** sign at this stage – **Currency** format is discussed shortly.)

3. Delete the row labelled **Petrol**.

4. Enter a label, **Total**, on the right of the label **Week4**. Enter a formula to calculate the **Total** spent on **Food** for all four weeks.

5. Replicate the formula used for calculating the **Total** spent on **Food**, for each of the other items, **Heating**, **Electricity**, **Rent, Petrol** and **Car**.

6. Save the spreadsheet with a name such as **Spending2**.

7. Insert a new column after **Week4** and before **Total** with the heading **Week5**. Enter the following data in the **Week5** column: **Food 53.97, Heating 31.29, Electricity 13.14, Rent 109.00, Petrol 25.42, Car 45.11**.

8. Calculate the **Total** spending in **Week5**.

9. Check that the figures for **Week5** have been included in the new figures in the **Total** column.

10. Save the spreadsheet with a name such as **Spending3**.

11. Print a copy of the spreadsheet.

Formatting a Spreadsheet

Excel has many formatting features to change the way text and numbers are displayed in the cells. The main formatting effects are accessed from the Excel 2007 Ribbon in the **Font** and **Alignment** groups on the **Home** tab, as shown below.

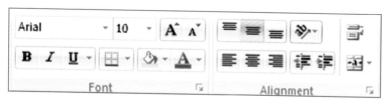

Labels and numbers can be aligned in the cells in several ways — left-aligned, centred and right-aligned. Vertical alignment can be at the top, middle or bottom of the cell.

Characters can be displayed in a range of fonts or styles of

lettering, in different sizes. The font size can be increased or decreased quickly using the letter **A** shown on the right above.

Bold, italic and underline effects may also be applied.

The general method is to select (i.e. highlight) the required cell or group of cells. Then select the required effect from the Excel 2007 Ribbon shown above.

The three icons shown on the right and in the **Font** group above enable you, reading from left to right, to put various borders round cells, fill cells with colour and change the colour of text. A large variety of cell borders is available after clicking the small arrow to the right of the border icon, as shown in the small extract on the right.

Selecting Cells for Formatting or Editing

Selecting a single cell

Click anywhere in the cell.

Selecting a group of cells

Hold down the left mouse button and drag the cursor over the required area of the spreadsheet.

Selecting a single row

Click in the box containing the row number on the left of the worksheet.

Selecting a single column

Click in the box containing the column letter **A,B,C,** etc., (or letters such as **AA**, **AB**,..... **ZZ**, etc.) at the top of the worksheet.

Selecting multiple rows or columns

Hold down the **Ctrl** key while clicking the required row numbers or column letters.

Selecting the entire worksheet

Click in the box containing a triangle in the top left-hand corner of the sheet.

In the example below, columns **C** and **D** and rows **5** and 6 have been selected. Once selected, any of the formatting effects, such as letters in italics or numbers in **Currency** format, can be applied to the highlighted cells.

D1		▼	f_x	
	A	B	C	D	E
1					
2			Weekly Spending		
3		Week1	Week2	Week3	Week4
4	Food	49.57	41.21	51.89	49.99
5	Heating	23.42	25.48	24.44	28.89
6	Electricity	11.33	8.88	9.95	12.11
7	Rent	97.00	97.00	97.00	97.00
8	Petrol	18.49	17.12	21.21	19.82

Formatting Numbers

Numbers can be displayed in several formats including *whole numbers* and *decimal* as well *currency* and *date*. Numbers are formatted using the **Number** group on the **Home** tab on the Excel 2007 Ribbon. Select i.e. highlight

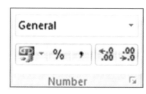

the numbers to be selected, as discussed on the previous page, click the arrow to the right of **General** shown above. This opens the drop-down menu shown in the extract on the right. The **General** format leaves numbers just as you type them in, while **Currency**

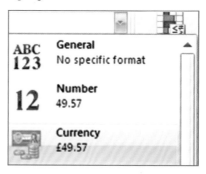

format adds a **£** sign and displays two decimal places i.e. two digits to the right of the decimal point. The icons shown below and under **General** above provide a quick way of changing the format of numbers. Reading from left to right, these are **Accounting Number Format**, **Percentage Style**, **Comma**

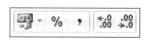

Style, (for separating thousands). The icons on the right above are **Increase Decimal** and **Decrease Decimal**, allowing you to increase or decrease the number of decimal places.

There are many other number formats available including **Date**, **Time, Percentages** and **Fractions**.

If you click the small arrow to the right of the word **Number** on the **Home** tab, shown on the right and in the

screenshot at the top of this page, the **Format Cells** dialogue box opens, as shown on the next page. This provides an alternative way to format numbers in selected cells.

The **Format Cells** dialogue box shown below provides tabs to alter the formatting of a spreadsheet. Apart from different number formats, you can also change the fonts, cell borders and fill colours.

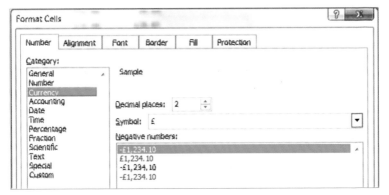

In the example below, Column **B** is in the **General** number format, Column **C** is in the **Accounting** format, **D** and **E** are in the **Currency** format. Column **F** has been set to have no figures after the decimal point. The numbers in column **F** have been inclined using the **Orientation** feature in the **Alignment** tab shown in the **Format Cells** dialogue box above.

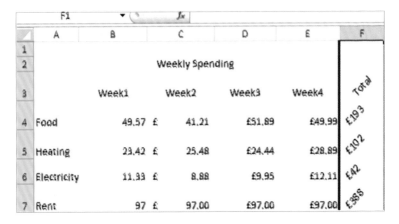

Exercise 3: Formatting a Spreadsheet

This exercise covers those features of Excel 2007 which allow you to change the appearance of a spreadsheet. All of the necessary skills are described in the previous pages. If you need help with a particular task, please refer back to the relevant section.

1. Reload the spreadsheet completed in Exercise 2, which you may have saved with the suggested name of **Spending3**.

2. Make a printout showing all the formulas used to calculate the **Total** spending column.

3. Display the data in the **Week1**, **Week2**, **Week3**, **Week4** columns to two decimal places (e.g. **247.87**). The figures in the **Total** column should be displayed without decimal places.

4. Change the font style, letter colour, cell borders and fill colours throughout the spreadsheet.

5. Save your spreadsheet with a name such as **Spending4**.

6. Print a copy of the spreadsheet on paper.

That completes all of the basic spreadsheet skills. On the next page there is a checklist of skills; you may wish to complete this list to assess your personal progress.

Checklist of Spreadsheet Skills

- Open a new spreadsheet
- Enter text
- Enter numbers
- Enter formulas by typing in a cell
- Enter formulas by selecting an Excel 2007 function
- Use replication
- Edit numbers and text
- Edit formulas
- Delete rows and columns
- Insert rows and columns
- Change the width of columns
- Change the alignment of text and numbers
- Change the style and colour of cell contents
- Apply different number formats such as Currency
- Save a spreadsheet as a file on a hard disc
- Retrieve a saved spreadsheet from a hard disc
- Print a spreadsheet on paper
- Display and print formulas

Excel Graphs and Charts

Introduction

Graphs and charts allow numbers to be analysed and compared at a glance; trends can be spotted and predictions made about the way things may develop in the future. Drawing graphs and charts by hand can be quite a difficult and time-consuming process; programs like Excel 2007 reduce the drawing of all sorts of graphs to a quick and simple operation involving a few clicks with the mouse. The basic method is as follows:

- The data to be used in the graph or chart is entered into an Excel spreadsheet.

- The numbers and labels to be "plotted" are selected i.e. highlighted in the rows or columns.

- The type of graph or chart required is selected from the wide choice available on the Excel 2007 Ribbon; for example, pie chart, column graph and line graph.

- Excel works out the scales for any horizontal and vertical axes and immediately draws the graph.

- Labels, titles, etc., can be added easily and the graph or chart is saved as part of the spreadsheet.

- The graph or chart can be printed separately.

- The graph or chart can be inserted into a report or other document in a word processor.

This chapter describes the use of Excel 2007 to create the main types of graphs and charts. Also explained is the insertion of a chart into a report in a word processor and printing a chart on paper. A practice exercise is included at the end of the chapter.

Types of Chart

The Pie Chart

The pie chart shows how different items in varying quantities contribute to a total. Various options are available to label the slices of the pie, including displaying the name of each item in the slice and the percentage of the total. A separate legend or key to the colours can also be displayed.

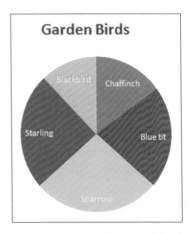

The Line Graph

The line graph shows how a quantity varies over a period of time. The time in weeks, months or years, for example is normally plotted along the horizontal scale with the quantity being measured on the vertical scale.

The Column Chart

This chart is useful for comparing quantities side by side; for example to compare the total weekly sales of different bar meals. You can alter the range of the scales and edit and format the titles, labels and text and background colours.

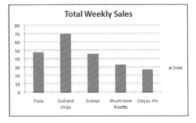

The methods for creating each of the above charts and graphs using Excel 2007 spreadsheets are discussed in more detail in the remainder of this chapter.

Drawing a Pie Chart

The data for this simple pie chart is entered into Excel 2007 as shown on the right.

	A	B
1	Garden	Birds
2	Bird	Number
3	Chaffinch	5
4	Blue tit	7
5	Sparrow	9
6	Starling	8
7	Blackbird	7

You can apply some colours to the text and backgrounds by clicking in the headers at the top of each row and on the left of each column. Then select a font

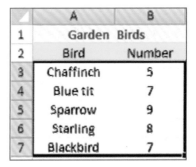

colour or a fill colour from the **Font** group on the Excel 2007 Ribbon with the **Home** tab selected.

Now, keeping the left mouse button held down, drag the cursor from cell **A3** to cell **B7**, so that all of the data is highlighted, as shown on the right. Do not include the titles in the selection area at this stage – they can be added later.

	A	B
1	Garden	Birds
2	Bird	Number
3	Chaffinch	5
4	Blue tit	7
5	Sparrow	9
6	Starling	8
7	Blackbird	7

Now click the **Insert** tab on the Excel 2007 Ribbon; as you can see on the **Charts** group below, there are icons for the various types of graph and chart such as **Column**, **Line**, **Pie** and **Bar**, etc.

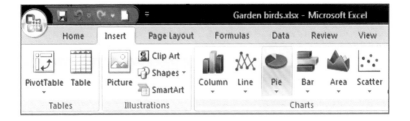

Now select the **Pie** icon from the Ribbon shown on the previous page and you can choose between various types of pie chart, as shown in the extract on the

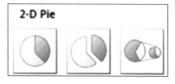

right. Click the type of pie chart you want and it instantly appears, embedded in the spreadsheet, as shown below.

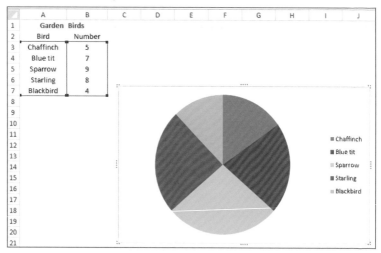

As shown above, Excel 2007 has included a legend or key to the right of the pie chart. This shows the colours Excel has used for each bird or slice of the pie. If you want to change the

colour of a slice, click the slice twice very slowly – not a normal double-click. Three small circles appear on the slice showing it is

selected. Now change the fill colour of the slice using the fill icon, shown left, found in the **Font** group on the **Home** tab of the Excel 2007 Ribbon. In the example on the right, the **Sparrow** slice has been changed to yellow.

Pie Chart Styles

If you click the **Design** tab while an Excel chart is highlighted in the worksheet, a huge choice of designs appears. These appear across the Ribbon in the **Chart Styles** group, as shown below.

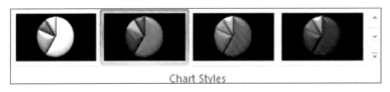

Chart Styles

The scroll bars on the right of the **Chart Styles** group above display many more sets of pie chart designs. The **Garden Birds** pie chart is shown below with one of the above **Chart Styles** applied.

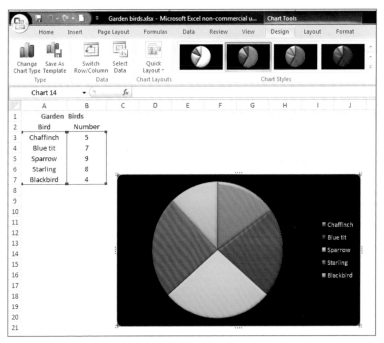

Changing the Layout of a Pie Chart

The **Quick Layout** feature in the **Chart Layouts** group on the **Design** tab on the Ribbon presents various options as shown on the left below.

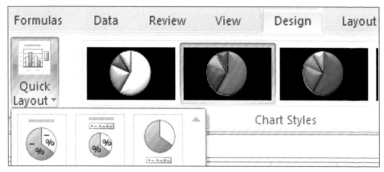

Options on the **Quick Layout** menu include the labelling of each slice as a percentage and hiding or displaying the legend, as shown on the right. The legend can be placed in various positions and these options are shown in full when you click **Legend** on the **Layout** tab of the Ribbon. You can also replace the default **Chart Title** with your own, such as **Garden Birds** shown on the right. The **Quick Layout** options also include displaying the data labels (**Chaffinch**, etc.,) inside of the slices as shown on the right. More options for the placing of data labels are given after you click **Data Labels** on the **Layout** tab on the **Ribbon**.

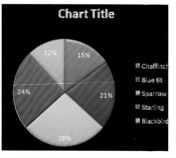

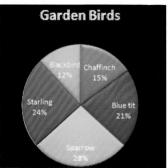

Updating a Chart

When a graph or chart is embedded in a spreadsheet as shown below, there is a live link between the data in the cells of the worksheet and the chart. If you make a change to the numerical data or a label in the spreadsheet, the graph or chart is automatically redrawn to reflect the new data or label.

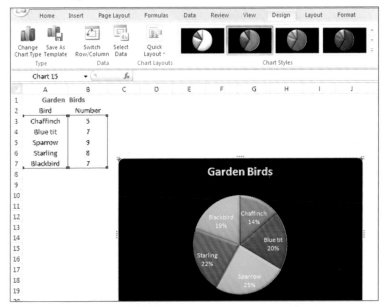

In the above example, the number for the **Blackbird** in cell **B7** is increased to **7**. The pie chart is automatically adjusted to show the new slices with the **Blackbird** slice increased to **19%** from **12%** as shown on the previous page.

Saving a Graph or Chart

Save the spreadsheet using **Save** or **Save As** from the **Office Button** menu as previously described. The graphs or charts will be saved on the hard disc as an integral part of the spreadsheet. When you later retrieve the spreadsheet from the hard disc, any graphs or charts will open up on the worksheet as shown above.

Drawing a Line Graph

The spreadsheet below shows a person's weight as they follow a dieting program for six months from January to June. Body Mass Index (BMI) is a measure of a person's weight in relation to their height; a BMI above certain limits suggests that a person may be classified as obese. The formula used to calculate BMI is as follows:

$$\text{BMI} = \frac{\text{Weight in Kilograms}}{(\text{Height in Metres}) \times (\text{Height in Metres})}$$

The **Height** squared i.e. multiplied by itself, is obtained by entering the formula **=C4*C4** in cell **D4**. This is replicated down column **D** by dragging the small cross from the corner of cell **D4**.

	A	B	C	D	E
1			Body Mass Index (BMI)		
2					
3	Month	Weight kg	Height (M)	Height Squared (M^2)	BMI
4	Jan	79	1.6	2.56	30.86
5	Feb	75	1.6	2.56	29.30
6	March	72	1.6	2.56	28.13
7	April	71	1.6	2.56	27.73
8	May	68	1.6	2.56	26.56
9	June	64	1.6	2.56	25.00

We could miss out column C and D and simply enter the formula **=B4/(1.6*1.6)** in cell **C4** since this person's height will always be **1.6** metres. However, the method in the above worksheet is more explicit and can easily be adapted for people of different heights and weights.

The problem now is to plot a line graph showing the months on the horizontal scale and the **BMI** on the vertical scale. To do this we first need to select or highlight the data in columns **A** and **E** only. This can't be done by simply dragging over Column **A** followed by Column **E**, since clicking and dragging in Column **E** deselects Column **A**.

Selecting Two Non Adjacent Columns

This is done by dragging the cursor down over cells **A3-A9**. Then holding down the **Ctrl** key and dragging over cells **E3-E9**. The extract below shows the **BMI** worksheet with the data and column headings in columns **A** and **E** highlighted and ready to be plotted.

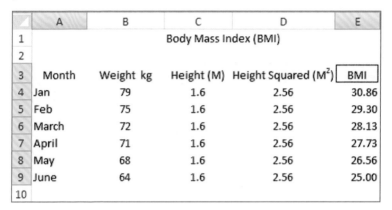

	A	B	C	D	E
1			Body Mass Index (BMI)		
2					
3	Month	Weight kg	Height (M)	Height Squared (M^2)	BMI
4	Jan	79	1.6	2.56	30.86
5	Feb	75	1.6	2.56	29.30
6	March	72	1.6	2.56	28.13
7	April	71	1.6	2.56	27.73
8	May	68	1.6	2.56	26.56
9	June	64	1.6	2.56	25.00
10					

Now select **Insert** from the Ribbon and choose **Line** from the **Charts** group as shown below.

Many different types of **Line** graph are available as shown on the menu extract on the right. This menu drops down when you click the **Line** icon shown above.

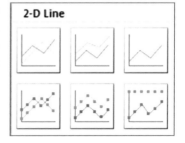

2-D Line

When you select one of the line graph types shown on the previous page, the graph appears instantly on the worksheet as shown below.

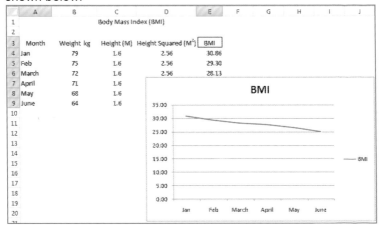

The first drawing of the line graph may not be what you want but it's not difficult to make modifications. For example, you might want to start the **BMI** vertical scale at **20.00**, say, rather than **0.00** as above. This can be done by selecting the Chart Area on the worksheet and then selecting

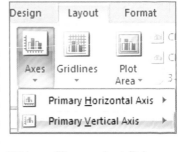

Axes from the **Layout** tab on the Ribbon. Then select **Primary Vertical Axis** and **More Primary Vertical Axis Options...**. From the **Format Axis** dialogue box which appears change the **Minimum** to **Fixed** and **20.0** as shown below.

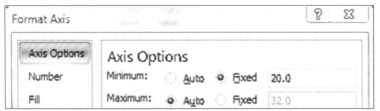

Formatting a Chart

The **BMI** line graph is shown below, automatically updated with the vertical scale starting from a **BMI** of **20.00** rather than **0.00**.

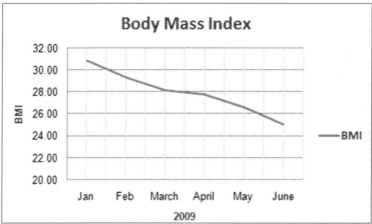

The above line graph has been formatted in a number of ways. To format a chart, first select the Chart Area on the worksheet as shown above. The icons on the Ribbon change to show the **Chart Tools**.

The above line graph has also been formatted to include a **Chart Title**. Initially **BMI** was inserted automatically from the selected **BMI** column in the spreadsheet. Click in the Chart Title area and type in the new title. Each of the areas in the chart above were first selected and then

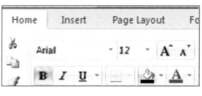

filled with colour using the fill icon on the **Home** tab shown above and right. Click the fill icon then select the required colour. The font colour in any of the text areas can be changed after clicking in each text area and then clicking the font color icon shown on the right, before choosing a colour.

Axis titles can be switched on or off after clicking **Axis Titles** on the **Layout** tab in the **Labels** group on the Ribbon. The **Chart Title** can also be switched on or off and its position altered.

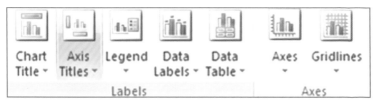

Clicking the **Gridlines** icon above on the right displays horizontal and vertical lines across the whole of the chart area, as shown on the line graph below and on the previous page.

Two Lines on One Chart

As shown below, Excel can display two lines, for example, **Weight** and **BMI**, on one chart. In the **BMI** spreadsheet shown previously, select columns **A**, **B** and **E**, highlighting the areas from row **3** to **9** inclusive, i.e. to include the column titles **Month**, **Weight kg** and **BMI**. As discussed earlier, selecting data in multiple columns which are not adjacent is achieved by holding down the **Ctrl** key while dragging with the mouse. Now click **Insert** and choose the type of line graph. The graph is displayed and can be formatted as previously described, as shown below.

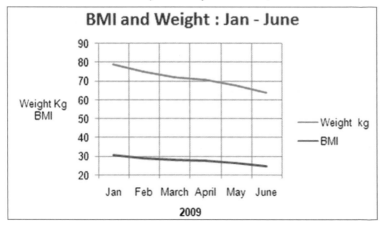

Drawing a Column Chart

This chart will be based on the **Bar Meals** spreadsheet shown below.

	A	B	C	D	E	F	G
1			Bar Meals				
2	Meal	Tues	Wed	Thurs	Fri	Sat	Total
3	Pizza	3	8	9	12	17	49
4	Cod and chips	7	6	14	23	21	71
5	Scampi	2	6	8	13	18	47
6	Mushroom Risotto	3	6	5	8	12	34
7	Coq au Vin	0	8	4	7	9	28
8	Total	15	34	40	63	77	229

A column chart for the sales **Total** in a week for each meal will make it easier to see the most popular dishes. We need to select the **Meal** column, Column **A**, by dragging the cursor from cell **A2** to cell **A7** only. Then keeping the **Ctrl** key held down, drag the cursor down the **Total** column, Column **G**, from cell **G2** to cell **G7**. Next select **Column** in the **Charts** group on the **Insert** tab on the Ribbon, shown below.

You are presented with a choice of many different designs for column charts as shown in the small sample on the right.

After you click on a column chart design, the chart immediately appears on the worksheet, a shown on the next page.

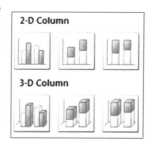

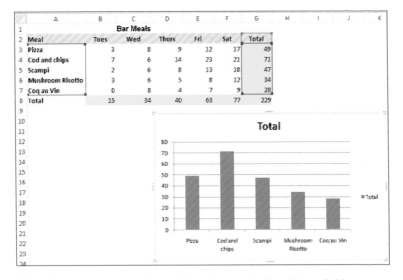

The chart can now be formatted after selecting it by clicking anywhere in the Chart Area above. Formatting the column chart with a **Chart Title**, **Axes Titles**, **Gridlines** and different colours for the text and fill areas is the same as described in the previous section for the **Line Graph**. The **Bar Meals** column chart is shown below after adding titles and formatting.

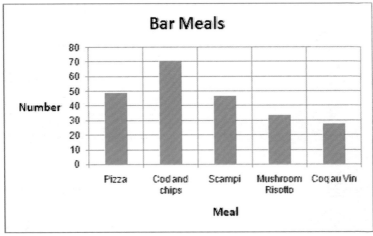

Changing to a Different Type of Chart

You might decide that another type of chart is more appropriate for your data; this is accomplished using the **Change Chart Type** icon on the left of the **Design** tab on the Ribbon shown below.

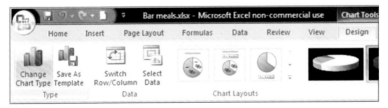

For example the **Totals** for the **Bar Meal** sales in the previous column chart could quickly and easily be presented as a 3-D pie chart, as shown below. Simply click the **Change Chart Type** icon shown above and select the new chart from the menu which appears, as shown in the small extract below.

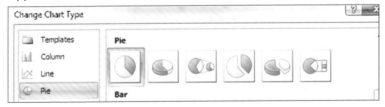

The **Bar Meals Totals** are shown as a 3-D pie chart below.

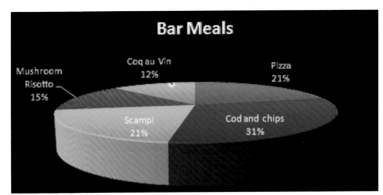

Drawing a Clustered Column Graph

This graph will show the sales of each meal side by side on the different nights. It is drawn after selecting all of the meals for every day. This can be achieved by dragging diagonally from cell **A2** to cell **F7** as shown in the example below.

	A	B	C	D	E	F	G
1			Bar Meals				
2	Meal	Tues	Wed	Thurs	Fri	Sat	Total
3	Pizza	3	8	9	12	17	49
4	Cod and chips	7	6	14	23	21	71
5	Scampi	2	6	8	13	18	47
6	Mushroom Risotto	3	6	5	8	12	34
7	Coq au Vin	0	8	4	7	9	28
8	Total		15	34	40	63	77	229

The clustered column graph is drawn after selecting **Column** on the **Insert** tab in the **Charts** group on the Ribbon. The icon for the clustered column chart is on the left of the group of three shown here on the right. When you select this icon the clustered column graph appears, as shown below after some formatting.

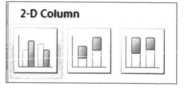

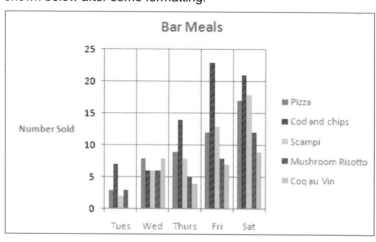

Printing a Chart

Although the chart appears to be an integral part of the whole worksheet in Excel, the chart can be printed separately. Select the chart by clicking anywhere in the Chart Area. Now click **Print** on the **Office Button** menu displayed by clicking the orb, as shown on the right, at the top left-hand side of the screen. The **Print** dialogue box appears as shown below. The radio button next to **Selected Chart** should be switched on, indicating that only the chart will be printed.

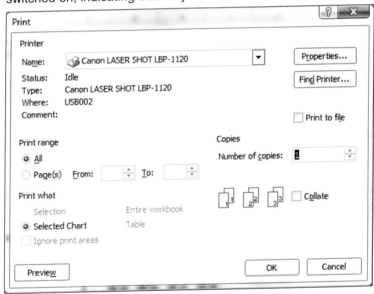

Click the **OK** button above to commit the chart to paper. To print both the spreadsheet table and the chart, don't select the chart on the worksheet. The **Print** dialogue box will then show **Active Sheets**, as shown on the right. If a chart or spreadsheet is too wide for the paper, switch to **Landscape Orientation** after selecting **Properties** shown above.

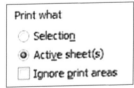

Inserting an Excel Chart into a Report

A report produced in a word processor such as Word 2007 can be illustrated by inserting graphs and charts from Excel 2007. In earlier times this would have to be done by drawing the graphs in by hand or perhaps by literally cutting and pasting with scissors and glue. As discussed shortly, the electronic process of inserting an object is still called "cutting (or copying) and pasting" although now it's all accomplished with a mouse and keyboard.

The word processor document should be open and minimised on the Windows Taskbar at the bottom of the screen. The **Bar Meals** spreadsheet should be displayed on the screen with the Chart Area selected and highlighted as shown below.

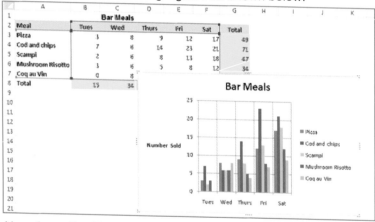

Now from the **Home** tab on the Excel 2007 Ribbon, click the **Copy** icon shown highlighted below the scissors on the **Clipboard** group shown below.

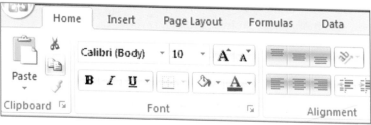

This places a copy of the **Bar Meals Chart** on the *Clipboard*, a temporary storage area from where it can be pasted into another program such as the Word 2007 word processor.

If the report is already open in the word processor but minimised, open the report on the screen by clicking **Bar Meals Review** on the Windows Taskbar as shown below.

Otherwise launch the word processor and open the report with the cursor placed roughly where the top left-hand corner of the chart is to go. Now click the **Paste** icon on **Home** tab on the Word Ribbon. The chart is pasted on to the report as shown below. In Word 2007 you can adjust the final position of the chart by selecting the **Format** tab and choosing a **Position** as shown in the small sample on the right. Otherwise the position of the chart can be adjusted by dragging with the mouse.

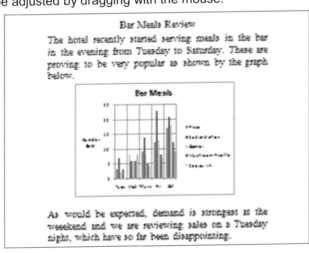

Exercise 4: Excel Graphs and Charts

The table below shows second-hand car sales in a local dealer's.

Make	July	Aug	Sept
Ford	7	9	6
Peugeot	5	5	3
Toyota	8	4	7
BMW	3	4	2
Honda	4	5	4
Renault	2	3	5

1. Enter the above data into an Excel worksheet.

2. Add an extra column, **Total**, after **September** and complete this column using the Excel SUM function and replication.

3. Save the Excel worksheet.

4. Create an Excel pie chart showing how the sales of each make of car contribute to the total sales.

5. Print just the pie chart without the spreadsheet table.

6. Create a clustered column graph showing the months along the horizontal axis with columns for all of the makes, as shown below. (You may need to click **Switch/Row Column** on the **Design** tab).

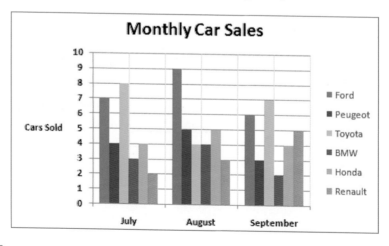

Using Excel as a Database

Introduction

The main use of spreadsheets is to automate calculations on large tables of figures and enable charts and graphs to be drawn easily. However, the layout of the spreadsheet in organized rows and columns makes it very easy to enter and create on disc a simple database such as a file of names and addresses. Once entered and saved in Excel, the names and addresses can easily be updated by amending details or adding new people. Excel 2007 also allows the sorting of records into order and the filtering of records containing particular information. This might for example, be useful for:

- The secretary of a club, group or society keeping membership details and sending out regular newsletters.

- A business sending out invoices, special offers, etc., to customers and clients.

- An organization wishing to keep personal details of staff or students, etc.

- Anyone sending out a lot of invitations, greetings or Christmas cards, etc.

An Excel address file may be used as the data source for importing a large number of names and addresses into a mail-merge program in a word processor such as Microsoft Word 2007. This allows address labels to be printed very quickly, saving a great deal of time compared with manual methods.

Creating an Address File in Excel

From **Start**, **All Programs** and **Microsoft Office**, select **Microsoft Office Excel 2007** as previously described.

After you've used Excel the first time it can subsequently be launched directly from the main **Start** menu. Excel opens ready for you to start entering the column headings, such as **First Name**, **Surname**, **Address Line 1**, **Address Line 2**, etc., as shown in the extract below. The column headings **First Name**, **Surname**, etc., play an important part in the mail merge, as will be seen later.

	First Name	Surname	Address Line 1	Address Line 2	Address Line 3
4					
5	John	Walker	19 London Rd	Lewes	E Sussex
6	Susan	Slater	Highfield	Milwich	Stone
7	Jill	Austin	Hinckley Farm	Radbourne	Derby
8	Robert	Burns	14 Belmont Rd	Murrayfield	Edinburgh
9	Sarah	Mitchell	Salmon Leap	Norham	Northumberland
10	Bob	Smith	71 Church St	Greenwich	London
11	Mike	Brunt	83 Valley Rd	Thetford	Norfolk
12	Jean	Baker	Westmead	Weaver View	Lichfield
13	Samuel	Johnson	The Cottage	Great Cubley	Ashbourne

You'll probably need to extend the width of the columns to accommodate the column titles and also the data. To do this, allow the cursor to dwell between the column headers. The cursor changes to a small cross, shown between **D** and **E** below. The cross can then be dragged to give the correct column width, while holding down the left mouse button.

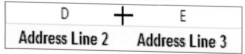

Entering the Data

It's simply a case of typing the names and addresses into the cells. *Don't use commas or punctuation marks* within an address field; "83, Valley Rd", for example, might cause problems. To move to a new cell press the **Enter** key to move down and the **Tab** key to move across.

Text can be formatted in the cells in Excel in a similar way to text in a word processor; the Ribbon in Excel contains the usual text formatting tools, bold, italic, underline, etc., as shown below.

To edit the data in a cell, double-click the cell. To format an entire row or column, first click the row or column header (**1, 2, 3**, etc., and **A, B, C**, etc.,) to select the row or column.

Saving the File of Names and Addresses

Click the **Office Button** in the top left-hand corner of Excel and select **Save As** from the drop-down menu. The file is saved as an **Excel Workbook** with the file name **Address List.xlsx** in this example, entered in the **File name** slot, as shown below.

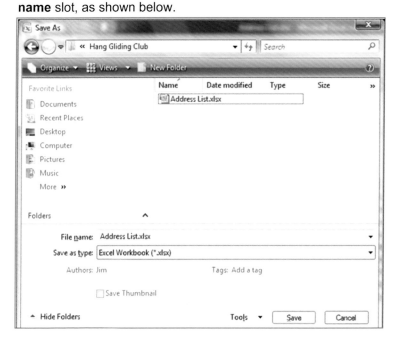

Make a note of the location where the address file is saved; you will need to browse for this file shortly when you carry out the mailmerge in Word 2007. In this example I have used the **New Folder** option, shown above on the **Save As** menu bar, to create a folder **Hang Gliding Club**. The full path to the data source for the mail merge is therefore:

C:\Hang Gliding Club\Address List.xlsx

Sorting into Order

To sort the address file into a particular order, such as alphabetical order of surname, drag the cursor over the names so that they appear highlighted. Don't include the column label or it will appear somewhere in the sorted list. Now select **Sort & Filter** from the right of the Excel Ribbon on the **Home** tab. From the drop-down menu shown on the right, choose the order you want to sort into, such as **A to Z**. A **Sort Warning** then appears from where you should select **Expand the**

selection and click **Sort**. Alternatively click **Custom Sort...** then choose the column you want to sort on from the drop-down menu as shown below.

The address file is shown below, with the records sorted into alphabetical order of surname.

4	First Name	Surname	Address Line 1	Address Line 2
5	Jill	Austin	Hinckley Farm	Radbourne
6	Jean	Baker	Westmead	Weaver View
7	Mike	Brunt	83 Valley Rd	Thetford
8	Robert	Burns	14 Belmont Rd	Murrayfield
9	Samuel	Johnson	The Cottage	Great Cubley
10	Sarah	Mitchell	Salmon Leap	Norham
11	Susan	Slater	Highfield	Milwich
12	Bob	Smith	71 Church St	Greenwich
13	John	Walker	19 London Rd	Lewes

An address file might contain hundreds of records and great savings in time can be made compared with sorting manually.

Using an Excel Filter

If you select **Filter** from the **Sort & Filter** menu shown on the previous page, you can remove certain records from the file. A small arrow appears at the top of each column. Clicking this displays a list of the data in the column; to remove a record from the file simply click in the box to remove the tick. In the example on the right, when you click **OK** the records for **Bob**, **Mike** and **Sarah** will be temporarily removed from the address list. These records can be reinstated later if required using **Clear Filter** from the drop-down menu.

Find & Select

This feature is found on the right of the Excel 2007 Ribbon on the **Home** tab. **Find & Select** allows you to quickly find certain text or cells with certain formatting such as italics or text or fill colour. The cursor jumps to each occurrence of the specified text or formatting and allows you to change it.

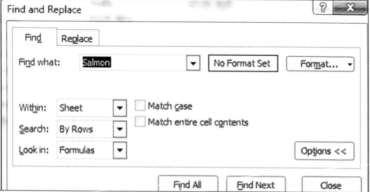

For example, entering the word **Salmon** in **Find what:** shown above, quickly moves the cursor to that cell, allowing it to be edited. Clicking the **Replace** tab above allows you to move to all occurrences of the specified text or formatting; these are replaced by the text or format in the **Replace with:** bar.

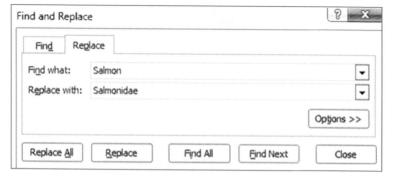

Using Excel as a Data Source

The address file just described can be used to infill names and addresses into a standard letter and to print address labels.

The standard letter, or mail merge, involves sending the same basic letter to many different people; each copy of the letter is personalized for individual recipients, so that one letter might start "Dear Mike" while another would begin "Dear Jill", together with their corresponding addresses.

There are two main components of the mailmerge:

- The basic skeleton of the letter which is the same for everyone.
- A list of names and addresses saved as a separate file, often referred to as the *data source*.

The list of names and addresses is first created and saved as a separate file in Excel 2007 as previously described.

After creating the Excel file, the basic letter is then typed in Word 2007, including a set of *placeholders* or *mail merge fields*. These are marked locations in the standard letter into which the individual names and addresses will be placed.

The mailmerge then takes place, during which individual names and addresses are copied from the Excel file into each unique copy of the letter. Finally the individual letters are printed.

The place holders in the standard letter must correspond exactly with the column headings in the Excel worksheet, i.e. **First Name**, **Surname**, **Address Line 1**, **Address Line 2**, etc., as shown in the extract below.

	A	B	C	D
3	**First Name**	**Surname**	**Address Line 1**	**Address Line 2**
4	Jill	Austin	Hinckley Farm	Radbourne

The above column headings are shown in position as place holders in a standard letter on the next page.

High Peak Hang Gliding Club
Roaches House
Leek
Staffordshire
ST6 5BY

29 June 2008

«First_Name» «Surname»
«Address_Line_1»
«Address_Line_2»
«Address_Line_3»
«Address_Line_4»
«Address_Line_5»

Dear «First_Name»

National Over 50s Hang Gliding Championship

This year we will again be fielding a team in this prestigious event; if you
would like to be considered for selection, please reply to me by letter at the

The position of the above place holders can be adjusted by dragging to give the layout you require. Word 2007 then allows you to preview the letters with the individual names filled in before printing on paper.

Printing Name and Address Labels

The Excel 2007 address file can also be used for printing address labels in Word 2007. A4 sheets of sticky labels are available and these have a reference number, such as Avery L7163. This is entered into the Word **Labels** feature and the Excel place holders

«First_Name» «Surname»
«Address_Line_1»
«Address_Line_2»
«Address_Line_3»
«Address_Line_4»«Address_Line_5»

«Next Record»

are applied to the labels. Once set up the **Mail Merge** feature can easily be used to print hundreds of labels using an Excel 2007 spreadsheet as the data source.

Managing Excel Files

Saving an Excel File

An Excel spreadsheet (called a workbook) is saved on a hard disc using **Save As** from the **Office Button** menu discussed earlier.

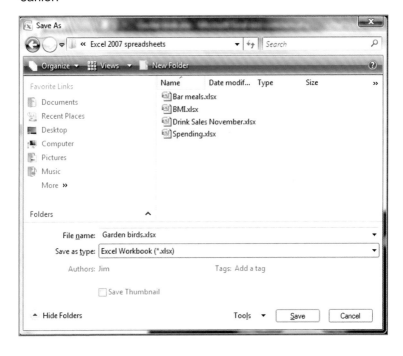

You make up a name for the file, such as **Garden Birds**, and type it in the **File name** slot shown above. In the above example the folder name **Excel 2007 spreadsheets** was selected by browsing the hard disc after clicking **Computer** shown on the left above.

Creating a New Folder

To make a new folder, first select the location where the new folder is to reside. This might be at the top level on the **C:** drive (hard disc) or within another folder. Click **Computer** shown previously, find the required location and click **New Folder**.

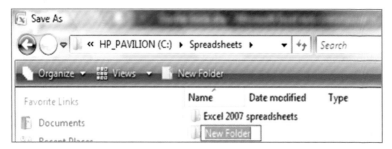

In the example above a new folder is being created within an existing folder called **Spreadsheets**. Overtype the words **New Folder** with your own name. If the new folder were called **Accounts**, for example, the address or path to this folder would be **C:\Spreadsheets\Accounts**.

File Types

An Excel 2007 spreadsheet is, by default, saved as an **Excel Workbook** as shown below. You don't need to type in the file name extension, **.xlsx** – it's added automatically.

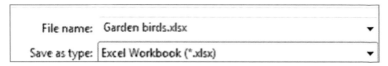

Although most users will probably only use the **Excel Workbook (*.xlsx)** format for saving files, many other formats are available after clicking the arrow on the right of the **Save as type:** bar shown above. These include the popular **PDF (.pdf)** or **Portable Document Format** used for Internet files and also several formats compatible with Apple Macintosh Computers.

Locating an Excel File

After you click the **Save** button on the **Save As** dialogue box shown previously, the Excel file is stored on your hard disc in the location, i.e. folder, which you specified. It's a good idea to try to create a logical system of folders with meaningful names so that you can easily find a spreadsheet, perhaps weeks or months after you created it.

To locate a file, first double-click **Computer** on the **Start** menu (Windows XP users should click **My Computer**), then browse on the appropriate disc drive, usually **C:**, for the required folder.

Files representing some of the small sample spreadsheets discussed earlier in this book are shown below in the **Computer** feature; in this view the file name and file name extension (**.xlsx**) appear alongside of the Excel 2007 icon.

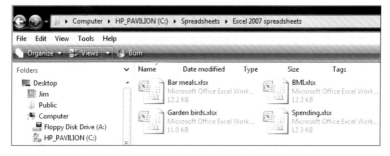

From the above extract from the **Computer** window, you can see that the full path to a spreadsheet file such as **Garden Birds** is:

C:\Spreadsheets\Excel 2007 spreadsheets\Garden birds.xlsx

Viewing Files in the Computer Window

The **Views** menu shown on the right allows you to display the Excel files in several different ways, including different sizes of icons up to **Extra Large**. If you want to find out more about the files, select **Details** from the **Views** menu on the right. The **Computer** window, as shown below, then displays the date and time when a file was last modified (or created, in the case of a brand new file).

The date and time when a file was last modified is useful because you often need to make sure you are working with the latest version of a file, copies of which may be stored on several different computers. The spreadsheets listed above can be sorted into alphabetical order of **Name**, **Date modified** or **Size**. This is done by clicking the title of the column such as **Name** or **Date modified**. In the example below the files have been sorted by **Date modified**.

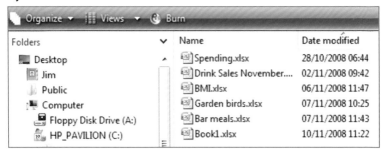

Common File Management Tasks

There are many tasks which are often needed on files in the **Computer** window, such as copying, moving, deleting and renaming. As usual Windows Vista provides several alternative methods to achieve the same task. For example, there are two Menu Bars on the **Computer** screen, which both have menus to carry out basic file management operations. These are the **Edit** and **Organize** menus on the two Menu Bars shown below.

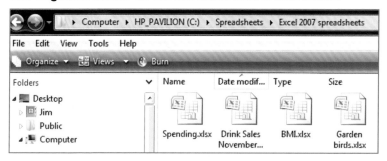

Right-Click Menus

A very quick and easy way to access Windows menus is to right-click over the file name. This displays the menu shown on the right. (Right-click menus are available in Windows programs in general).

Clicking **Norton 360** allows you to scan the selected file with the well-known anti-virus and Internet security program. **Rename**, not surprisingly, allows you to type in another name for the file.

Properties of an Excel file are discussed at the end of this chapter. Common tasks on the file name right-click menu are described on the next page.

Open

Opens the selected spreadsheet in Excel 2007. A file can also be opened in Excel by double-clicking the file name.

Print

Opens the selected spreadsheet file and prints a copy on paper.

Send To

Allows you, for example, to copy the file onto a CD, send it in an e-mail and place an icon for the file on the Windows Desktop.

Copy

Places a copy of a selected file on the Windows Clipboard; a copy of the file remains in the original location. To copy the file to another folder, right-click over the new folder in the **Computer** window. Then select **Paste** from the menu which appears.

Cut

Removes the spreadsheet file from the current folder and places a copy on the Windows Clipboard ready to be pasted into another folder as described above.

Create Shortcut

Places an icon for the file on the Windows Desktop. Double-click this icon to quickly launch Excel with the spreadsheet file open.

Delete

This removes the selected file to the Windows **Recycle Bin**. (From where it may be retrieved if the bin hasn't been emptied).

Using Drag and Drop

Files may also be copied or moved in the **Computer** window by keeping the *right-hand* button held down and dragging the file icon over the new folder. Release the right-hand button and select **Copy Here** or **Move Here** from the pop-up menu.

Copy Here

Move Here

Create Shortcuts Here

Cancel

Properties of an Excel File

To find out more details about a particular file, highlight the file in the **Computer** window as shown on the previous page, then select **Properties** off the **Organize** menu. The **Properties** window opens as shown below, in this example displaying the details of the **Bar meals** spreadsheet discussed earlier.

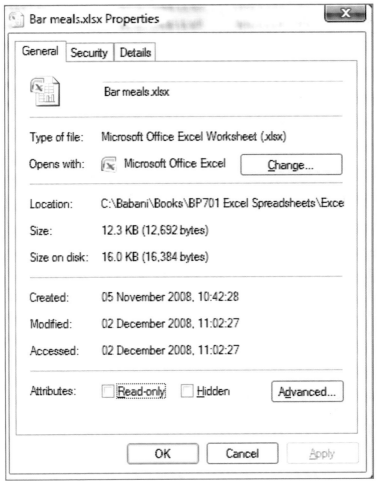

Read Only Files

If you were worried about accidentally deleting a copy of a very important file you could set it to **Read-only**, as shown on the **Properties** window on the previous page.

Hidden Files

If you have some Excel files which are confidential you can hide them so they are not listed in the **Computer** window shown earlier. Anyone who knows the name of a hidden file can still open it in Excel after clicking **Open** on the **Office Button** menu and typing the file name in the **Open** window.

To hide a file, first click the square next to **Hidden**, as shown on the **Properties** window on the previous page and then click **Apply** and **OK**. Now click **Tools** on the **Computer** Menu Bar and select **Folder Options...** as shown below.

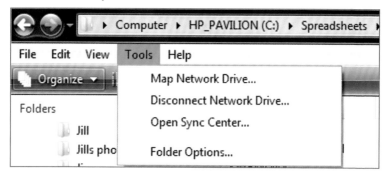

Next select the **View** tab in the **Folder Options** dialogue box and make sure **Do not show hidden files and**  **folders** is switched on as shown on the right. Click **Apply** and **OK** and the hidden file will not appear next time the **Computer** window is opened. Only people who know the name of the file will be able to view and open it using **Open** off the **Office Button** menu in Excel 2007.

Safety Precautions

Introduction

After using Excel 2007 for a while you'll probably have created some large and useful spreadsheets and saved them as *files* on your hard disc. These files may contain important financial or confidential personal data. Unfortunately there are many ways that spreadsheet files may be lost or damaged, for example:

- You might accidentally delete the wrong file or a malicious person might delete files deliberately.

- You can easily delete the latest version of a file in a "drag and drop" operation by accidentally overwriting the new file with an older version.

- A powercut, electrical surge, spike or computer error might damage files which are currently in use.

- You can damage files which are currently open if you don't follow the correct procedure to shut down your computer.

- You might forget the location on your hard disc where a particular spreadsheet file was saved.

- A file may be corrupted, requiring the hard disc to be reformatted so that all of your data files, including Excel files, are wiped.

Fortunately there are many effective and inexpensive ways to safeguard your Excel files and these are discussed in the remainder of this chapter. (External threats to your files are discussed in Chapter 10).

Making Regular Backups

If you've spent a lot of time building large Excel files, it's essential that you make backup copies. These should be on a separate removable storage medium such as a CD, DVD or flash drive. Making a duplicate copy of a file on the same hard disc is of little use if the computer or hard disc is stolen or damaged. The backup copy should be kept in a different physical location from the computer. Should the original copies of your Excel files be lost, you can restore the backup copies and continue working. Otherwise you may be faced with retyping entire spreadsheets.

Backup Media

For the home or small business user, cheap media such as CDs and flash drives have simplified life considerably. Below is a backup procedure which has served me well in the production of numerous books using Word files – so far avoiding the loss of a single file. Backing up Word files is essentially the same as backing up Excel spreadsheets.

- Regular daily backups of current work in progress are copied onto a removable USB flash drive, which is overwritten each day with the latest file. The flash drive is much faster and holds much more data than the floppy discs formerly used.

- Weekly backups are copied onto CD-Rs, which now cost only a few pence each. One CD-R can easily store several books like this one and very many Excel spreadsheets. Files on a CD-R cannot be deleted.

Checking that a Backup File is Retrievable

It's always a good idea to check that the backup was successful by opening the copies of the files from the backup medium. This can be done from within Excel using **Open** on the **Office Button** menu or by double-clicking the file name in the **Computer** window as discussed in Chapter 8.

CD Writing or "Burning"

Earlier versions of Microsoft Windows did not include CD writing or "burning" software, so it was necessary to purchase a third-party product. Two of the most popular packages are Easy CD Creator from Roxio and Nero from Ahead Software. The CD burning software built into Windows Vista is an extremely useful backup tool and now includes the ability to write data on DVDs.

Using Windows Vista's CD/DVD Burning Software

The method of copying files to a CD or DVD is basically the same and is described on the following pages. First a blank disc is placed in the drive and after a very short time the **AutoPlay** window opens as shown below. From this window select **Burn files to disc**.

The following **Burn a Disc** window appears, with a drop-down menu allowing you to choose a formatting option for the new disc. To open this menu click the arrow next to **Show formatting options**. If you are using a CD-R disc which can only be written to once, click the radio button to the left of the word **Mastered** shown below.

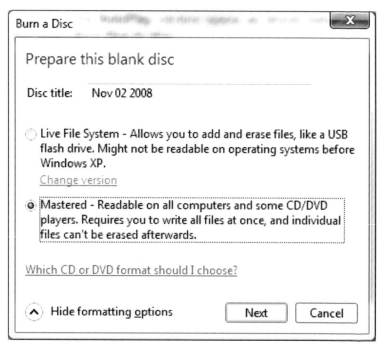

Click **Next** and a **Computer** window opens asking you to drag the required files onto the CD/DVD drive (frequently drive **E:**), as shown on the next page.

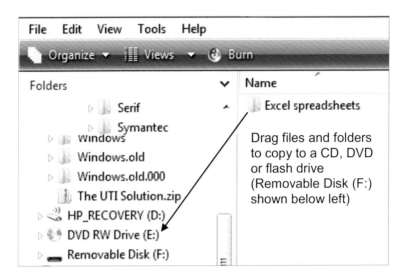

After you have dragged the required file or folder and dropped it over the **E:** drive (or perhaps **D:** or **F:**), a balloon appears on the Taskbar at the bottom of the screen, as shown on the right.

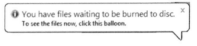

When you click the balloon, the files or folders to be copied are displayed at the top right of the **Computer** window as shown below. Now click **Burn to disc** off the toolbar, as shown below.

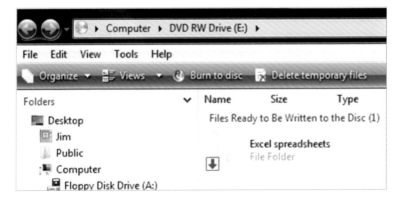

The **Burn to Disc** dialogue box appears, with an option to add your own **Disc title** instead of the current date used by default.

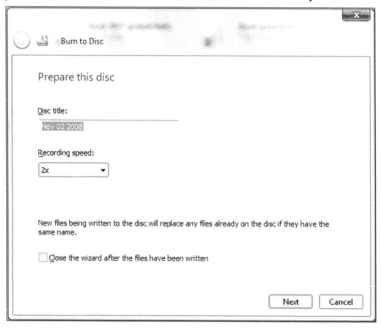

Click **Next** and the actual burning and copying process begins. After a short time the following dialogue box appears, stating that the burn was successful and giving you the chance to copy the same files onto another disc. Click **Finish** at the bottom of the dialogue box to eject the disc.

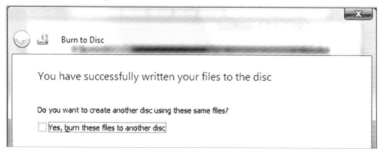

Checking the Files on a Backup CD

Copying files and folders to CD (or DVD) has, in my experience, always been extremely reliable. However, to check that your backup is an exact copy (and that you have copied the right files), place the disc back in the drive. The **AutoPlay** menu may pop up, with an option to **Open folder to view files**. Or the **Computer** window may open automatically, showing any folders on the disc, such as **Excel 2007 spreadsheets**, shown below.

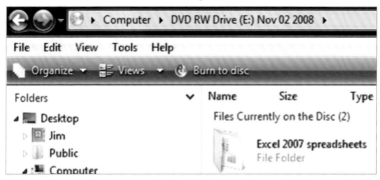

Double-click a folder to check its contents, such as the **Drink Sales November.xlsx** file shown below. Then double-click the spreadsheet file to open it in Excel.

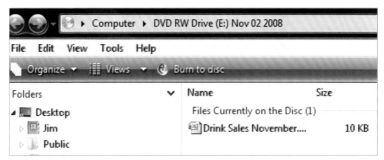

To check the date a file or folder was modified, etc., select **Views** form the Menu Bar above and then click **Details**.

The USB Flash Drive or Memory Stick

These devices are an extremely fast and convenient form of storage. They are a type of a *dongle*, a small device which plugs into one of the USB ports on the computer. The USB ports are usually two or four small rectangular slots on the back and sometimes also on the front of the computer.

A flash drive appears in the **Computer** window as a **Removable Disk**, usually designated **(F:)**, **(G:)** or **(H:)**, etc., depending on what other storage devices are fitted to your machine, as shown below and on the next page.

Removable Disk (F:)

The USB flash drive is very easy to plug in and remove and, being roughly the size of a little finger, is extremely portable. Being a USB device, the flash drive can be "hot-swapped", i.e. plugged in and detected while the computer is up and running.

The USB flash drive can be used as a form of backup storage and is available in a range of sizes from 256MB to 5GB with prices starting from just a few pounds for the smaller versions.

Obviously if you need to build up a large *permanent archive* for all of your spreadsheets or music or photographic files, for example, a number of CD-Rs or DVDs is a safer solution. However, the USB flash drive is ideal for anyone on the move, wanting to move files quickly between laptop and desktop computers or share files with friends or colleagues in a fast and easy fashion. As mentioned earlier, I use flash drives, (also known as "memory sticks"), to make quick daily backups. As the flash drive can be written to many times, each day the latest files *overwrite* the earlier versions. For complete safety, every week permanent archive copies of the files are made to CD or DVD as described in the previous section.

Recovering Files from a Flash Drive or CD

Both USB flash drives and CD/DVD drives appear as additional devices in the **Computer** window, shown below and accessed from the **Start** menu.

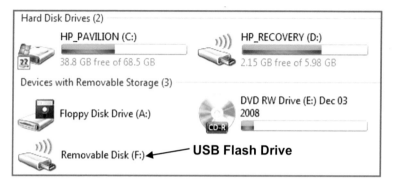

If you need to recover the files you've backed up onto a flash drive, CD or DVD, etc., place the removable medium in the computer. Start up the program used to create the file, in this case, Excel 2007. Now click the **Open** option off the **Office Button** menu. Select the required drive (**E:**, **F:** or **G:**, etc.) and then click the folder, in this example **Excel 2007 spreadsheets**, from the drop-down menu under **Folders** shown below.

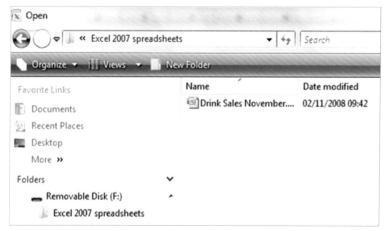

95

Select the file **Drink Sales November** in the **Open** window shown on the previous page and then click the **Open** button at the bottom right of the window. The spreadsheet **Drink Sales November** should now be displayed on the Excel 2007 screen as shown below.

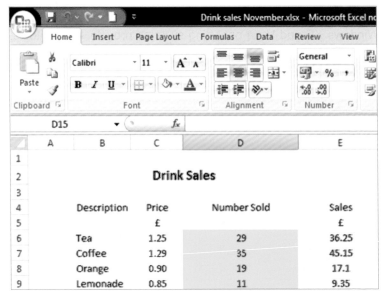

Another way to open a file from a hard disc, CD or DVD (or any other disc or medium such as a removable USB flash drive) is as follows. Display the file name, e.g. **Drink Sales November** in the **Excel 2007 Spreadsheet** folder shown previously, in the **Computer** feature.

If you double-click a file name such as **Drink Sales November** or its icon, as shown above, the file will be opened in the program which created it, Excel 2007 in this case.

The following pages discuss some "housekeeping" tasks to ensure that your computer keeps running efficiently. If it develops a hardware or software problem you may, in the worst case, need to have your hard disc wiped and the software and data files (such as spreadsheets) will need to be re-installed, all being well using easy-to-find backup copies, as described earlier. The Windows XP and Vista operating systems provide several tools, i.e. utility programs, to help maintain the efficiency of your computer.

Disk Cleanup – Removing Redundant Files

During normal running, your computer creates a lot of temporary files on the hard disc. When you browse the Internet, the content of Web pages is saved so that the site can be viewed more quickly at a later time. When using programs like Excel 2007, a lot of temporary files are created. These take up disc space and if ignored for a long time may cause the computer to run slowly.

To remove these redundant files cluttering up your hard disc, run **Disk Cleanup**, once a week say, by selecting **Start**, **All Programs**, **Accessories**, **System Tools** and **Disk Cleanup**.

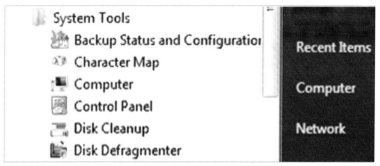

After you've used **Disk Cleanup** once, in future the program can be launched directly from the main **Start** menu. A window opens giving you the chance to clean up just your own files or the files of all users of the computer.

After making a selection, you choose the drive you wish to clean up – usually drive **(C:)**. **Disk Cleanup** then takes a few minutes to calculate how much disc space can be saved by deleting unnecessary files.

After calculating the potential gain in recovered disc space, the unnecessary files are listed, as shown below.

When you click on an entry, such as **Temporary Internet Files**, the purpose of the files is explained in the **Description** panel as well as guidance on the effects of removing them.

Decide which files to delete and mark their check boxes with a tick. The amount of free disc space to be gained is displayed in the window shown on the previous page. When you've marked which files are to be deleted, click **OK** and the window shown below appears.

Click the **Delete Files** button shown above to complete the cleanup operation.

You can quickly check the free space on your hard disc by click-ing the **Start** orb, then click **Computer** off the **Start** menu. The extract from the **Computer** window below shows that the hard disc drive **(C:)** initially had **24.0GB** free space. After running **Disk Cleanup**, the amount of free space increased to **24.2GB**.

Using Disk Defragmenter

After you've been using your computer for a while, many files will have been repeatedly modified and resaved. The original files and the changes may become separated, scattered about the hard disc in different places. This will impair the performance of the computer when it tries to open a file which is spread around many different locations; *defragmentation* is a process which rearranges the hard disc to make it run more efficiently. In Windows Vista, the **Disk Defragmenter** program is scheduled to run automatically. Alternatively it can be launched by clicking the **Start** orb then selecting **All Programs**, **Accessories**, **System Tools** and **Disk Defragmenter**.

After you've used **Disk Defragmenter** the first time, the program can be launched in future by clicking its name, which by now will be listed on the **Start** menu.

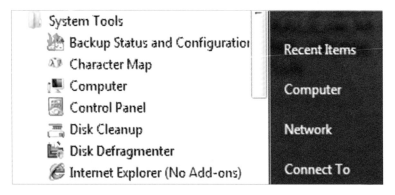

The **Disk Defragmenter** window opens, as shown on the next page. In this particular example, the **Disk Defragmenter** program has been scheduled to run once a week, but you can change this if you wish after clicking **Modify schedule…**.

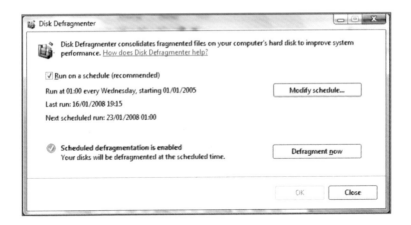

Please also note in the **Disk Defragmenter** window above, the **Defragment now** button allows you to manually start an immediate defragmentation whenever you think it might be beneficial. Select the drive you wish to defragment, usually **(C:)** then click the **Defragment** button.

The defragmentation process may take several minutes or a few hours, depending on the size and state of the hard disc. Fortunately you can continue to use the computer while the **Disk Defragmenter** program is running.

Good Housekeeping

It's recommended that, in order to keep your computer running efficiently, **Disk Cleanup** and **Disk Defragmenter** are run regularly – at least once a week, especially if the computer is heavily used. If the computer appears to be running slowly for no obvious reason, it may be worth carrying out a manual defragmentation.

System Restore

This feature takes a "snapshot" of the critical settings in Windows and other software on your computer. It does not make copies of your *data files* such as Excel spreadsheets, so you should still make backup copies as described earlier. **System Restore** saves a collection of critical settings known as a *restore point*. Restore points are scheduled to be saved automatically or you can make one at any time manually by clicking the **Create** button in **System Protection** within **System Restore**.

If something goes wrong with your machine, perhaps after installing new software or hardware, you can revert to a restore point made at a time when you know the computer was working well. The computer will then have the same settings as it had at the time of the chosen restore point.

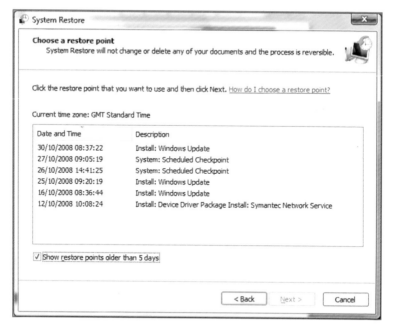

Windows Update

This feature, launched from **Start** and **All Programs**, enables you to download from the Internet the latest modifications to the Windows software and install them on your computer. Such modifications, often called "patches", might, for example, be intended to close a breach in the security of the Windows operating system. This could potentially allow "hackers" to gain access to your computer and possibly steal financial or personal information.

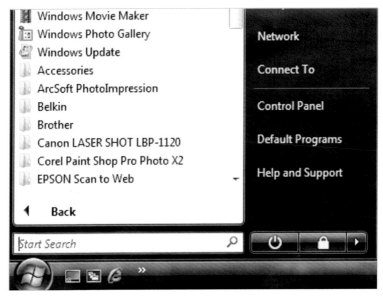

You can schedule your computer to check for updates at a certain time every day. Updates are downloaded from a Microsoft Web site; you are told which updates are available and can choose whether to download and install individual updates to your machine. When version 11 of the Windows Media Player was launched, it was available for downloading as an automatic update for users of Windows XP. (The Windows Media Player version 11 is provided as standard in Windows Vista).

Summary: Safety Precautions

- Always make backup copies of important spreadsheet files. Use a removable storage medium such as CD, DVD or flash drive (memory stick).

- Label the backup copies and store them safely.

- Check that the backed up files can be retrieved and opened in Excel 2007.

- Use the Windows **System Tool**s, **Disk Cleanup**, **Disk Defragmenter,** to remove redundant files and optimize storage on your disc.

- Use **System Restore** to overcome software problems; the computer is returned to an earlier configuration, saved at a time when the computer was working correctly.

- Make sure **Windows Update** is switched on so that the latest Windows software modifications are downloaded to your computer from the Internet.

- Obtain a plug-in surge protector, costing £5-£10, to prevent surges or spikes in the electricity supply from damaging your computer and its hard disc. Some extension leads have built-in surge protectors.

- Any cut in your electricity supply or surge in power can cause loss of data and possible damage to equipment. An *Uninterruptable Power Supply (UPS)* provides instant battery power so that data can be backed up or the mains power restored. A UPS may also give protection from power surges. UPS devices for home or small business cost £30-£110.

- Always finish a session using **Shut Down** on the right of the **Start** menu. Simply switching off the computer or the power point can damage files which are open.

External Threats to Your Excel Files

Introduction

This chapter continues with the task, started in the last chapter, of safeguarding your Excel files; the following pages concentrate on threats to your files from the outside world. Even though your computer is apparently sitting safely in your home or office, there are plenty of threats to your files from outside – largely due to the Internet and wireless broadband, as outlined below.

- A "hacker" might gain access to your computer and copy important files such as Excel spreadsheets.

- A virus might attack your computer and destroy files or even wipe the entire hard disc.

- You may be using an *unsecure* wireless router for your Internet connection. Other people nearby can detect your network, use your Internet connection and intercept information being sent and received.

- Your Excel files may be stored on a laptop computer, a flash drive, "memory stick" or a removable hard drive; these may be lost or stolen.

- The computer might be damaged in a fire or flood.

Windows Vista and XP have several built-in software features to protect your files from external threats and there are numerous other products from third party suppliers. These are discussed in the remainder of this chapter.

The Windows Security Center

You can carry out an audit of all the security features in Windows by launching the **Windows Security Center**. Click **Start**, **Control Panel** and double-click the **Security Center** icon as shown on the right. You are recommended to make sure that the main security features are either switched **On** or marked **OK** as shown below.

Security Center

In the **Windows Security Center** shown above, each of the main features, **Firewall**, **Automatic updating** and **Malware protection**, etc., has been expanded to give more information. This is done by clicking the downward pointing arrowhead,  as shown here on the right. In the **Security Center** as shown above, click the upward pointing arrowhead to collapse each security feature.

The Windows Firewall

The firewall is a piece of software or hardware designed to protect your computer from criminal activity such as hackers or fraudsters. Windows has its own firewall which should be turned on, unless you have installed an Internet security package which includes a firewall, such as Norton, F-Secure or McAfee.

Turning Windows Firewall On

Select **Start**, **Control Panel**, then double-click **Windows Firewall** and click **Change settings**. If necessary click the circular radio button to make sure **Windows Firewall** is **On**.

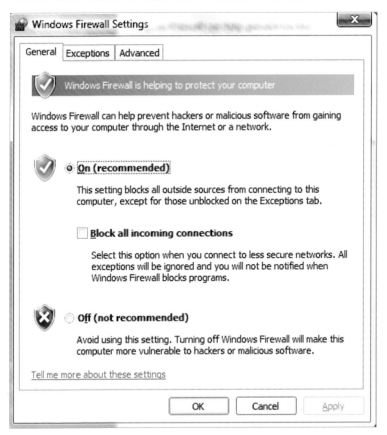

Automatic Updating

Windows Update provides regular modifications to the Windows operating system; these are often designed to make the system more secure and take the form of a small piece of software or "patch". **Windows Update** allows you to schedule your computer to check for the latest updates and download them to your computer from the Internet. Sometimes completely new versions of a major Windows component such as the Windows Media Player may be available as an update.

Windows Update can be launched initially from the **Start** menu, then **All Programs** and **Windows Update**. The next time you want to use **Windows Update** it can be launched directly from the main **Start** menu. As shown below, the **Windows Update** screen opens and displays the update status of your computer.

As shown above, you are informed when **Windows Update** last checked for available updates and the date when updates were actually installed. Clicking **Check for updates** above on the left-hand side allows you to carry out an immediate, unscheduled check for available updates.

Change settings, shown on the left of the image above enables you to schedule automatic daily or weekly checks for updates.

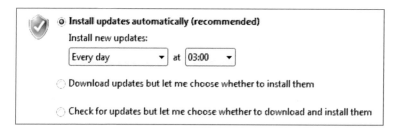

The radio buttons (circles) above allow you to choose whether you want automatic installation of updates or to control the downloading and installation yourself.

Clicking **View update history** shown on the left of the image on the previous page shows the updates that have been installed on one particular computer. The list can be scrolled to view almost an entire year of updates.

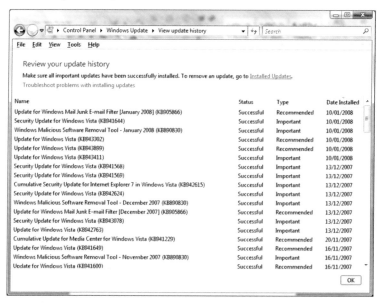

Malware Protection

Malware is an abbreviation for malicious software and refers to computer viruses and other malevolent programs; the computer virus is a small program written for the purpose of causing damage and inconvenience. In the worst case it might cause the contents of a hard disc to be wiped.

The **Malware protection** extract from the **Windows Security Center** shown above reports on any anti-virus software installed on your computer. It's essential that you have an anti-virus program installed and that this is regularly updated so that it can detect and render harmless the latest viruses.

Well known anti-virus software includes Norton AntiVirus, McAfee VirusScan, F-Secure Anti-Virus and AVG Anti-Virus. Many companies also produce complete Internet security packages which include anti-virus software as well as firewalls and protection against *spyware* – software designed to collect personal information from a computer.

Anti-virus/Internet Security packages typically cost £20 – £40 and this includes the software CD or DVD and a year's updates of virus definitions. Updates are normally downloaded automatically from the Internet. Many companies now allow one software package to be legally installed on up to three computers. Subscriptions to an anti-virus package are normally renewed annually.

Norton 360

Norton 360 provides total protection for your files in a single package. This includes anti-virus software as well as protection from hackers and "spyware". Spyware is illegal software installed on your computer via the Internet. This can monitor your Web surfing, alter settings and take control of some aspects of your computer. Norton 360 can be bought for under £60 and may be installed on up to 3 computers running Windows Vista or XP.

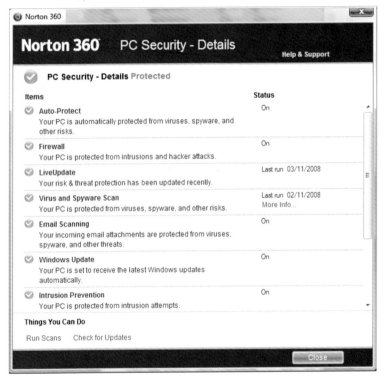

As shown above, Norton 360 protects files from viruses and there is a **Firewall** to keep out hackers. As new viruses are discovered, the Norton 360 database of known viruses is automatically updated on your computer via the Internet.

AVG Anti-Virus

This software, available for Windows Vista and Windows XP, can be obtained as a free 30-day trial download from the AVG web site at **www.avg.co.uk**. As can be seen below, it includes a **Firewall**, **Anti-Spyware** and **Anti-Virus** protection with automatic updates to enable it to recognise the latest viruses. There is also **Anti-Spam** protection to filter out unwanted and fraudulent e-mails.

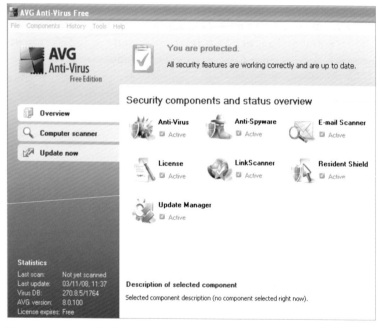

You can upgrade from the trial version of AVG Anti-Virus to the full version for £39.99, at the time of writing.

Anti-virus programs normally carry out automatic scans at regular times which you can schedule; it's also possible to launch a manual scan whenever the need arises.

Wireless Network Security

Wireless broadband routers have greatly improved most people's Internet experience but, without adequate precautions, your network of one or more computers may be ***insecure***. This is because anyone, such as a near neighbour with a wireless-enabled computer or someone in the street with a wireless laptop, may be able to detect your network and use your Internet connection. As shown below, my computer has detected my **BTHomeHub** plus two networks belonging to neighbours. One of these is about 30 metres away and is listed as an **Unsecured network** in the **Connect to a network** feature in the **Windows Network and Sharing Center**, as shown below.

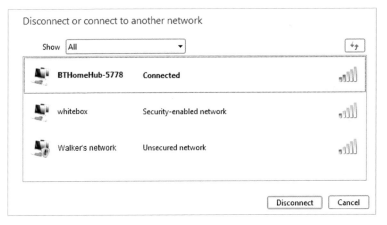

Although a firewall should stop anyone getting access to your computer and its files, it's possible for a determined hacker to intercept your network "traffic", including for example, Excel 2007 files which you have e-mailed.

Making a home or small business network secure usually involves setting up a *wireless key*, or password. Also data files (such as Excel spreadsheets) are *encrypted* i.e. scrambled to make them incomprehensible to any hackers eavesdropping within the range of your wireless network signals.

Summary: External Threats to Your Files

- Use the **Security Center** in Windows Vista and XP to turn on the **Windows Firewall** to prevent hackers from getting access to your files. Alternatively install a firewall from a 3rd party company as part of a complete Internet security and anti-virus package.

- Make sure that **Automatic Updates** is turned *on* in the **Windows Security Center**, so that you automatically receive the latest modifications intended to improve Windows security.

- Install anti-virus software which is regularly updated to detect and eradicate the latest viruses.

- If you are using a wireless broadband router, make sure it is a *secure network* which uses *encryption* and requires *wireless security key* to gain access. Otherwise people nearby can eavesdrop, share your Internet connection and intercept your data.

- The Web site for the manufacturer of your router should explain how to make your network secure.

- If possible, try to locate your computer and backup media in secure situations where there is minimal risk of theft, floods or fire. Install a smoke alarm in rooms where computers or backup media are kept.

- When travelling with a laptop computer or with removable media such as CDs, memory sticks or removable hard drives, take care to ensure that important files are not lost or stolen.

Glossary of Spreadsheet Terms

Alignment   The position of text or data in a cell – left, right or centred and top, bottom or middle.

AutoSum   An icon giving access to various mathematical functions, such as total and average.

Backup   A duplicate copy of a file, to be used if the original is lost or damaged.

Cell   Small box on a spreadsheet which can contain a number, label or formula.

Cell reference   The column and row headings which locate a cell on a spreadsheet table or grid, e.g. **D9**.

Chart   A diagram allowing sets of numerical data to be compared, e.g. pie chart and column chart.

Clipboard   An area of memory used to hold data temporarily during copying and "cut and paste" operations.

Computer   A window used to display and manage the discs, folders and files on a Windows Vista computer.

Drag and drop   Holding down the left-mouse button to move a screen object then releasing at the new position.

Excel 2007   The World's leading spreadsheet program.

File   A spreadsheet or other document saved on a magnetic medium such as a hard disc.

File type   The format used to save a document such as a spreadsheet, e.g. *.xlsx for an Excel workbook.

Folder   The electronic equivalent of a wallet file.

Font (Fount)   A style and size of letters, e.g. *Arial 10 italics*.

Format Painter   A "brush" tool for copying the style and layout of text or numbers from one cell onto another cell.

Format   The style, colour and alignment of text plus currency signs and decimal places in numbers.

Formula Bar	A rectangle at the top of a spreadsheet, allowing the entry and editing of formulas in a cell.
Function	A formula which can be selected from the Ribbon, such as Total or Average.
Gridlines	Vertical and horizontal lines on a spreadsheet.
Label	Text used as a heading for a set of data.
Office Button	Spherical icon at the top left of the screen, which launches the main menu for saving, printing, etc.
Office 2007	Suite of Microsoft software including Excel 2007 and Word 2007 and various other programs.
Quick Access Toolbar	Small row of icons at the top left of the Excel screen, for tasks such as Save, Undo, New.
Recalculation	If a number in a cell is changed, any dependant calculated cells are corrected automatically.
Replication	Copying a formula down a column or along a row, automatically amending the cell references.
Ribbon	A rectangular bar across the top of the Excel 2007 screen containing numerous tool icons.
Right-click	Clicking the right-hand mouse button to produce menus relevant to the current cursor position.
Save	Storing a spreadsheet on a hard disc, etc.
Spreadsheet	A grid of cells or small boxes containing numbers, labels or formulas, enabling rapid calculations and easy drawing of charts.
Windows	Operating system for a PC computer, providing the "user interface" of windows, icons and menus. XP and Vista are the latest versions.
Worksheet	Another name for an Excel spreadsheet.
Workbook	A set of several Excel worksheets saved and displayed as a single file. Worksheets are accessed by tabs at the bottom of the screen.

Index

A

Activation	12
Address file	72
Address labels, printing	78
Alignment in cells	45
Anti-virus software	111
Automatic Updating	108
AutoSum	29
Average function	33
AVG Anti-Virus	112

B

Backups	88-96

C

CD Burning	89
Cell	1
contents	21
editing	26, 39
reference	1
selecting	46
Chart	
inserting in report	68
printing	67
updating	57
Column chart	52, 63-65
Column, widening	21
Computer window	82

D

Data source	77
Database	7, 71
Deleting	
column	41
row	40
Disk Cleanup	97
Disk Defragmenter	100

E

Editing spreadsheet	39, 44
Excel 2007	9
installing	10
launching	13
Ribbon	14
screen	14
Excel files	85
managing	79-86
saving	79
viewing	82
Excel filter	75

F

File types	35, 80
Files	
locating	81
recovering	95
Flash drive	94
Folder, new	35
Format Painter	16
Formatting	
chart	61
numbers	47
spreadsheet	45, 49
text	45
Formula Bar	23, 24, 31, 39
Formula	6
displaying	23, 30, 37
entering	22
Formulas Tab	17
Functions	26

G

Graphs and charts	51
Gridlines, printing	37

H

Home Tab   16

I

Insert Tab   17
Inserting
   new column   43
   new row   42

L

Labels, entering   21, 28
Landscape orientation   36
Line graph   52, 58-62

M

Malware protection   110
Memory stick   94
Mistakes, recovering from   41
Moving
   along a row   20
   down a column   19
   to a specified cell   20
Multiplying cells   5, 25

N

Names and addresses   7, 71
New folder   35, 80
Norton 360   111
Numbers entering   22, 28
Numbers formatting   47

O

Office 2007   9
Office Button   15, 35
Office Help   15

P

Pie chart   3, 52, 53-57
Portrait orientation   36
Printing spreadsheet   36
Product Key   10

R

Recalculation   2
Replication   30, 32
Ribbon   14
Right-click menus   83

S

Save As   35, 79
Selecting separate columns 59
Sorting into order   74
Spreadsheet   1
   advantages   8
   applications   4
   formatting   45
   moving around   19
   printing   36
   saving   34
   skills   50
SUM function   24, 29
System Restore   102

T

Totalling   4, 24, 29, 31

U

Undo feature   41
Updating a chart   57

W

Windows
   Firewall   107
   Security Center   106
   Update   103
Wireless network security   113
Workbook   18, 35
Worksheet   18, 35
   moving around   19